The Twenty-Minute

LIFETIME

A Guide

To Career

Planning

By Gavin A. Pitt

Prentice-Hall

The Twenty-Minute
Lifetime

The Twenty-Minute Lifetime

A GUIDE TO CAREER PLANNING

GAVIN A. PITT

**Vice President, The Johns Hopkins University
and The Johns Hopkins Hospital**

With Assistance of

RICHARD W. SMITH

Englewood Cliffs, N. J.

PRENTICE-HALL, INC., 1959

To My Wife
ELEANORE

PREFACE

ONE OF THE greatest losses of human resources in the United States results from the fumbling process by which all too many college graduates determine their careers. As a result, they may lose five or more valuable years drifting from one job to another.

During the more than fifteen years that I was associated with business and industrial organizations, I talked with hundreds of young college graduates, many of whom had no concept of what type of career they wished to follow. These interviews suggested the need for an interpretive guide that would describe opportunities in the modern complex corporation and treat such fields as education, government service and the professions.

Within the last two decades the college graduate has come into his own in America's business and industrial organizations. Recruiters from hundreds of companies now roam the college campuses looking for the most promising seniors. Often there are so many seniors to be seen that the recruiter is limited to a twenty-minute interview with each student. And in those twenty minutes, with little or no information about a particular company or about other opportunities which might better fit his interests and abilities, a senior may make a decision that will affect his lifetime.

It is hoped that *The Twenty-Minute Lifetime* will prove helpful to college students and recent graduates as they make the most important decisions of their lives.

I am indebted to the leaders of some of the largest industrial and commercial organizations in America for their contributions concerning future opportunities in their fields.

I wish to express my gratitude to Miss Anne Knell for her assistance in preparing the final manuscript.

BALTIMORE, MD.   GAVIN A. PITT
1959

CONTENTS

The Twenty-Minute

Lifetime

CHAPTER ONE

THE TWENTY-MINUTE
LIFETIME

THIS SPRING, as in all other springtimes since the late 1940's, a swarm of well-dressed, soft spoken, serious men will descend upon college campuses all across the country. At each college or university they will spend one, two, or three days closeted in a spare office or an empty classroom talking earnestly to a long line of sometimes confused, sometimes determined, sometimes bewildered, but always eager college seniors.

The College Recruiters

These men are the college recruiters, employed by the great—and sometimes the small—industries and business firms of America to locate and to hire the talent that their employers require to staff their ever-growing and ever more capable complex organizations.

To many college seniors, the pleasant fellow in the conservative business suit, the Oxford button-down collar, and the "sincere" necktie represents the first real contact with the world of the giant corporations. For the student, still burdened with courses in thermodynamics, monetary economics, or the history of humanism, the great names of General Motors, Boeing, Minneapolis-Honeywell, and the Prudential Life Insurance Company belong to glamorous denizens of another world—the world outside the ivy walls of alma mater.

At Princeton, Gonzaga, Emory, Michigan State, California, Brown, or Kenyon, the scene is the same. The college recruiter from the Big Corporation smiles pleasantly, extends his hand and introduces himself to the college man entering his office. The student smiles self consciously, gingerly takes a seat, and nervously accepts a proffered cigarette. The stage is set.

Briefly the recruiter outlines the background of the Big Corporation. Plants in seven states—leader in electronics, textiles, atomic energy, and automotive fuel pumps—has a comprehensive training program for young men just out of college—is a fine place to work—has all the fringe benefits imaginable—and, best of all, Big Corporation is an outfit that favors youth. Big Corporation is looking for young men who are willing to work, have ambition, and are not afraid of a challenge.

The student sits listening to the recruiter in a daze of excitement. This fellow is talking about him.

"You say that you are getting a degree in Business Administration and a 'B' average?" asks Big Corporation.

The student nods, keeping his fingers crossed. He knows that he still has that Spanish Reading examination to take to clear his language requirement for graduation.

"Well," Big Corporation goes on smoothly, "I think that you will fit into our Philadelphia operation very nicely. They have a new training program up there for fellows like you. And, of course, you can go on to get your Master's Degree at the University of Pennsylvania at night. Big Corporation will pay the tuition costs."

The student looks—and is—bewildered. He fumbles for a second cigarette. "But, what will I do up there?" he finally asks.

The recruiter becomes quite serious. "You'll do just what you like to do and just what you do best," he says. He goes on to explain that the corporation training program gives young men a chance to see how they like a variety of assignments and how well they perform in a number of different departments. The young man then picks the job that suits him best at the end of the training period. The recruiter does his best to make the Big Corporation program sound very reasonable and, at the same time, very exciting.

The talk then turns to salary—when raises can be expected. The answer is logical if the man is good. Other details such as sick pay, vacation, and hospitalization are touched upon. Big Corporation also has a retirement plan, but that holds little interest for the twenty-two year old student.

The recruiter has made his points well. The student decides that he wants to work for Big Corporation. A starting date is agreed upon, and the student promises to report to the personnel department of the Philadelphia office on July 15th. The recruiter stands up, shakes hands with his new colleague, and the interview is over.

The entire discussion has lasted just twenty minutes. And, in that period of time, the student has committed himself to a career at Big Corporation—a career that could last a lifetime.

Two months later, the student—now a full-fledged college graduate—reports to Big Corporation and is assigned to filing cards in the production control office. Four months later he has shifted to the purchasing department and put to filling out routine forms. In another four months he finds himself in the fiscal control office shuffling papers and in a complete state of disillusionment. He wants to quit.

He thinks back to his four years of study and of the theories of high finance, business operation, and marketing that he worked so hard to master. Now he is using none of that information in his work.

And he thinks back to that twenty-minute interview, now hazy in his recollections, and he wonders what kind of gold brick was sold to him by that smooth talking college recruiter.

The answer to his musing is that he was *not* sold a gold brick. The recruiter did not lie to him. It is true that he showed Big Corporation in the best possible light, but he made no flagrant misstatements about the operation of the company and about what it could do for a college graduate.

The young man's problem is that, at the time he spent his fateful twenty minutes with the college recruiter, he was not in a position to properly evaluate what the recruiter was telling him, and this lack of "savvy" was compounded by his having no idea of what he, himself, wanted to do in the business world.

Your Future Career

This book is an attempt to make it possible for young men in college, and those just out of college who are still groping for a career in business and industry, to avoid the disillusionment experienced by the hypothetical senior described above. However, it should be clearly understood at this point that this book is not a treatise on vocational guidance. The selection of a lifetime career is a personal matter that must be left in the hands of the individual.

All that this book attempts to do is to point out the vital necessity of making a career choice as early as possible and to sketch a few outlines showing what a young man can expect, and what will be expected of him in the first few years of work in a variety of fields.

It is a rare young man who knows exactly what his life work is to be at the time he enters college, and it is not at all unusual for a college senior to step from the graduation platform with his diploma in his hands but without an idea in his mind concerning his future career. This is a truly tragic situation.

The young man without a clearly defined goal must spend literally years skipping from job to job in search of the type of work that will give him the satisfaction and the income that he needs. These wasted years, usually those between the ages of twenty-two and thirty, are never really regained by the individual. They represent a loss that, in personal terms, is deplorable and that, in national terms, is a needless waste of American manpower.

The period of a man's life between the ages of twenty-two and thirty is an energetic one. These are the years in which the young man has the confidence and the enthusiasm to tackle difficult tasks. They are the years in which he has the stamina to work long hours, to study late into the night. It is a time of life when his learning potential is still high. In short, it is the time of life when a man is best equipped physically and psychologically to prepare himself for a responsible position in business or industry.

These are the years in which the scholar earns his Ph.D. and begins his career—the years in which a lawyer attends law school and serves out his apprenticeship as a clerk in a law office—the years in which the doctor attends medical school and does his interning. These are the vitally important years to every man.

Yet many men squander this period in an aimless search for a career that will satisfy their interests and their talents.

And these lost years can never be regained. In today's America, the young man is being pushed into positions of responsibility as in no other time in the past one hundred years. Frank Pace, Jr., the president of General Dynamics, is forty-six years old. The Vice-President of the United States is forty-five and Senator Kennedy of Massachusetts is being seriously considered as a presidential candidate at forty-one.

These are not rare examples. Professional consulting firms whose job it is to find top caliber men to fill high executive positions in American industry are well aware of this quest for youth. The specifications handed them by their clients list the maximum age for a man to fill the president's chair of a large corporation at fifty. For an industrial vice-president, the age limit is often set at forty-five.

It is a matter of the most elementary arithmetic to discover that the young man who made a firm choice of a career at age twenty-two has eight more years of experience than has the man who accidently stumbled into his niche at thirty.

While American industry is demanding vigorous, relatively young men to fill its higher executive echelons, it is not willing to sacrifice experience in order to obtain youth. Future vice-presidents must have both. And the only way for a man to have both experience and youth is for him to have made a career choice at an early age.

Admittedly this is not an easy thing to do. Choosing a career is, in many ways, like choosing a wife. Both choices commit the man for life and mistakes can be most costly. Most of us, the movies notwithstanding, do not marry our childhood sweethearts, and most of us eventually outgrow our desires to be a fireman or a circus performer. There are, of course, a fortunate few who do marry the girl next door and who do become doctors after having made this career choice at the age of twelve. These are the lucky ones and the remainder of this book need not concern them at all.

But what of the undecided?

For them this is indeed a complicated world. There are literally thousands of careers from which to choose, and the choice is not limited to careers. The young man looking for a way to get ahead in the world must choose whether he is going to be a physicist or an electrical engineer. Having decided to become an engineer, he must decide whether to go into the aircraft or the appliance industry. Having chosen the aircraft industry, he must again decide between product engineering and production engineering. The necessity for choice does not stop here. Having chosen product engineering, the young man must again choose between a host of items that go into the modern aircraft or missile.

Eventually he finds himself an expert in the design of IF strips of UHF tracking receivers. Specialization has not made the selection of a career any easier for the young man.

The Specialization Problem

It is extremely difficult if not impossible for the college boy who decides to major in electrical engineering to know that, in ten years time, he is going to be very bored and very dissatisfied with an assignment that has him designing and redesigning a small, but important, section of an ultra-high-frequency radio receiver.

And this degree of specialization is not limited to the sciences. A personnel man may find that his work is limited to settling grievances arising out of different interpretations of a labor contract. A business administrative major may find that his work in industry has come down to filing progress reports with a government agency with which his company is doing business.

The college freshman or sophomore, observing an older brother, a neighbor, or a friend enmeshed in the web of industrial specialization may reject a career in engineering or personnel work. "I don't want to get stuck in the kind of rut that poor Harry is in."

This kind of reasoning can only make it more difficult for the young man to plot his future course. Specialization is with us to stay, and the current trend in our society indicates that we can expect an even higher degree of specialization in the years ahead. But there is an important corollary that must be remembered when talking about more intensive specialization. The very fact that there are going to be more and more experts toiling in ever narrowing fields means that the opportunities for the man of broad vision with administrative abilities that cut across many fields of specialization will be greatly increased.

One of the goals of this book will be to point out to the young man pondering his future the difference in careers that lead to severe specialization and those that lead to activities of a broader, more comprehensive approach to business and industry. This is not to infer that a specialized job is inferior to that of the administrator. For many men, great satisfaction can be obtained from intensive activity in a narrow field. In the sciences and in scholarship this is the way in which progress is made. But the young man should know enough about the ways of business and industry to be able to make his own choice. He should not, unknowingly, choose a path that will lead him into an area of specialization where he will be dissatisfied with both the type of work that he is asked to do and with the opportunities for advancement that are denied him because of this specialization.

There are many other pitfalls into which a young man in search of a career may fall, and this book will point them out.

Your Education

One of the basic assumptions of this book is that it is written for young men with, or in the process of acquiring, a college education. Within the last two decades, the A.B. and the B.S. have become the standard entrance requirement for positions in industry and business that eventually lead to top administrative posts. It is only a matter of time before the M.A. or the Ph.D. will become the minimum requirements. In government and in education, the advanced degree requirement is already firmly entrenched.

And for the ever more complex American industrial scene, a college education is not enough. Every year industry invests millions of dollars in training courses and in on-the-job training programs in quest of young men who, one day, will be capable of taking over the administrative posts of the major corporations. In almost every case, a college degree is required for admittance to these programs. The degree, while not infallible proof of a young man's intellectual ability, is the best yardstick presently at hand.

However, the businessman is not the only one with a stake in these training programs. The individual young man is also making an investment. He is investing two or more of his vitally important years. He has already been forced to use up two of these years in military service. A young man should select his industrial training course with the same care with which he selected his college. Later chapters will attempt to describe these training courses and to point out just what benefits a young man can expect to obtain from such a program. They will also point out what the corporation will expect of him. This information can save an eager young man from the kind of disillusionment experienced by the hypothetical college senior whose plight was described earlier.

Critical Decisions

The young man choosing a career must make two basic decisions. He must decide whether he is going to be an accountant or an advertising man, a salesman or a member of a personnel department. Having made this decision, he must then decide in what industry he is going to practice his profession. The second decision is every bit as important as the first. A wrong choice of industry can possibly negate all the work that has gone into the preparation for a specific career.

For example, great merchandising organizations such as Proctor and Gamble require a number of chemists. But the major emphasis in such an organization is on sales and promotion. The young man who chooses chemistry as a career should realize that in such organizations the top executive jobs are almost invariably filled from the sales, merchandising, and advertising departments. And that while it is true that a chemist can make an excellent salary at Proctor and Gamble, it is a path that does not often lead to the executive suite.

Here again the decision must be made by the individual. But, at the time the decision is made, the young man should have enough information upon which to make a sound judgment. This book will supply this information. Not all men are cut out to be administrators, and many are wise enough to realize it. However, should a young man's interests include both chemistry and a desire for administrative responsibility, he had best look for employment in some of the basic chemical companies, such as duPont or Olin-Mathieson, where the working chemist can aspire, with greater possibility of success, to a top administrative post.

Another decision that must be made by the young man starting out in the business world is the choice between a large corporation and a small company. Can a newcomer become lost in a big company? Are the chances for advancement in a small company limited? These problems will be discussed in detail in later chapters. The large corporation-small company debate is very similar to the big university-small college problem that faced the student upon graduation from high school. When both sides of the question have been weighed, the final decision will probably be made on the individual personality of the young man.

The book is not to be considered as a comprehensive guide to employment. Many important areas are not even discussed. There is no evaluation of the problems of the young farmer, the aspiring actor, or the struggling playwright. The book does contain a listing of American industries that will, in the coming decade, offer a wealth of career opportunities. It also outlines opportunities in government and education. The book will indicate what careers within each area offer the most chance for advancement.

Some of the evaluations may prove surprising. For example, the exciting field of atomic energy, while of vast importance, may not absorb large numbers of people during the next ten years.

There will be clear statements as to what personal and educational requirements are necessary for certain types of work. It will be pointed out, perhaps to some for the first time, that there is quite often a decided difference in the requirements of graduation and the requirements for success in the business and industrial world.

Nor will the price of success be sidestepped. Many jobs demand a great deal from the individual in terms of mental strain, after hours work, travel, and continual study. The rewards for such positions are usually high but the young man must decide whether or not he is willing to pay the price for the monetary gain that is offered.

These are the things that this book will attempt to make clear. There are a number of points that it will make no effort to cover. For example, there will be no attempt made to tell a young man how to do a particular job. There will be no value judgments placed on the various industries and careers described—no handy check list that will enable the young man to answer a few questions, total his score, and obtain an infallible guide to the future.

Decision making is always hard work, and this book will not make the choice of a career any easier. It will, however, make it possible for the young man to make a more intelligent choice based on a clearer understanding of what that choice will mean later in life.

Nor does the book contain any shortcuts to success. There is no mathematical formula that the bright young man can apply to insure his reaching the presidency of Big Corporation before the age of fifty. The closest that the book comes to such advice is in the statements made by outstanding executives in a great variety of industries. These men have generously contributed their time and their knowledge to the preparation of this book because they fully recognize the importance of young men finding their career or field of interest before it is too late for them to make substantial progress in it.

Only in the final chapter does the book offer any specific advice to the young man. And this chapter does not really make the choice of such a career any easier. It is simply a word of advice on how to make the most of that vital twenty-minute interview.

While based on the college recruiter-student interview, the book contains information that will be of value to anyone seeking his niche in the business world. It will outline the types of questions that he should pose to the company representative on the other side of the desk and indicate the type of answers that the interviewer wants to hear from the student. It will present a guide that will make it possible for the young man to make the most of what is quite often the twenty minutes that shape a lifetime.

CHAPTER TWO

OPPORTUNITIES
IN OUR COMPLEX
BUSINESS WORLD

WHEN THE foreign press wants to take a sly poke at the American way of life or, for that matter, when we want to make fun of ourselves, the easiest way to accomplish this objective is to caricature the American automobile. In its cartoon version, loaded with chrome, over-burdened with headlights and taillights, a block long, and with tail fins that scrape the sky, the motor car seems to stand out as a symbol of the American way of life.

Why?

Because in purely symbolic terms the automobile does stand for America. It is big, luxurious, and flamboyant and, in many ways, America is big, luxurious, and flamboyant. In the cartoon these features of American life are represented by the length of the car, the multiplicity of lights, the chrome, and the tail fins. But in a larger, more subtle sense the automobile does represent the America of today. The automobile means suburbia, afternoon bridge clubs, cross-country vacations, traffic jams, and super highways. It is difficult if not impossible to imagine what this nation of ours would be like without the automobile.

When the cartoons equate America and the automobile, the symbolism is extremely apt. If occasionally the details are a trifle exaggerated, it does not change the basic picture.

And, as the automobile symbolizes American social mores, the automobile industry symbolizes American industry. Perhaps no other industy—outside of the Federal government—utilizes as great a variety of skills and services as does the automobile industry.

11

One out of every seven gainfully employed people derive their livelihood from the automotive industry or from businesses operating in direct support of that industry.[1]

The automobile industry employs doctors and nurses by the hundreds to staff their plants; lawyers by the hundreds to negotiate contracts, compute taxes, and oversee their extensive patent and real estate holdings; teachers by the score to run training courses for assembly line workers and vice-presidents. Engineers and scientists have reached the position within the auto industry where they are housed in glass enclosed temples known as research centers.

To tell you that the industry employs accountants, personnel men, production control people, and experts in automation is to belabor the obvious—to point out that this same industry employs social scientists, marketing researchers, advertising men, and salesmen is not surprising—to explain that the manufacture and sale of automobiles also requires the talents of artists, creative writers, and psychologists may strain your credulity but should not shock you.

An Ideal Example—the Automotive Industry

Because of the great variety of professions utilized by the automotive industry, it is an ideal industry to examine in order to obtain a general picture of how an individual can find his career in the corporate world.

One out of six business firms in the United States is connected, in one way or another, with the automobile industry. And this collection of businesses runs the gamut from producers of raw material (steel) to straight retailing (automotive supply stores). Somewhere within this giant complex of industry is a career for every young man.

The question is "Where?"

In order to visualize the complexity of the auto industry, let us trace the origin of an automobile from its basic raw material to its sale on the showroom floor of a neighborhood dealership.

This is not as simple as it sounds. Because the development time for an automobile is from two to three years, it is a moot point whether the beginnings of a given automobile model is in the open hearth of a steel mill or in the open mind of a marketing researcher.

---

[1] All statistics in this chapter are taken from *Automobile Facts and Figures*, 1957 edition, Automotive Manufacturers Association, Detroit 2, Michigan.

Market Research

Years before an automobile is delivered to a dealer for sale to the public, a corps of marketing research people conducts literally thousands of interviews with the potential buyers in order to determine just what kind of automobile the public will want to buy in the years ahead. This kind of planning is extremely important. Mistakes can cost millions.

In the early 1950's, the Chrysler corporation bet on engineering and comfort instead of style and came very close to going out of business. By discovering tail fins in 1957, this same company was able to recoup much of its previously lost ground. Needless to say, its market research department is much larger today than it was ten years ago.

Once the general public opinion trend is measured by the marketing department and evaluated by the psychologists and the sociologists, the findings are forwarded to the engineering department and the design phase of the automobile gets underway.

At this point, it should be noted that while the automobile industry employs large numbers of people in its marketing research sections, its need for trained psychologists and sociologists is relatively small. The specialists in these fields who do find their way into the automotive field are extremely well paid, but the main market for their talents is still in the educational and governmental fields. The existence of well-paying jobs for a specialized career in any industry does not necessarily mean that this is the best point at which to begin such a career.

Research Engineering

Once the basic configuration of the proposed automobile is determined by the market research department, the engineers begin to translate this information into a finished design. While the market research crews have been out collecting data, engineering groups have been at work on a variety of mechanical problems. New engines, brakes, steering and springing mechanisms have been developed and tested.

Off in a remote corner of the research center, men have been exploring the possibilities of gas turbines and automatic guidance systems. Here again, a value judgment is in order. The automobile is primarily a product of practical engineering. While the industry uses product engineers by the hundreds, there is little room for the basic research scientist. True, the Detroit firms do employ men to engage in pure research—the development of new steel for engine blocks and the exploration of new uses for aluminum or on government contracts but the major employers of research scientists are outside of the automotive field.

Designing

The same marketing information that was given to the engineering department is simultaneously supplied to the designers. It is the task of the automotive designer to reconcile the desires of the public with the practical data developed by the engineer. No single industry employs great numbers of designers, but it is in the automotive field that this profession achieves, perhaps, its greatest recognition.

Production Engineering

When the final automotive design is agreed upon by engineering and industrial design (or styling, if you prefer), the problem is handed over to the production engineering teams.

The automobile is a mass-produced item, and the man who can find a faster, easier way to make a product will always be in great demand. The automotive industry requires large numbers of product and industrial engineers.

Production Control

With the mass-produced item also comes the need for production control men and a whole host of people who make sure that fenders, seats, steering wheels, and bumpers are available and that they arrive at the proper spot on the assembly line at the proper time. These jobs require men who are unafraid of detail, have a strong sense of urgency and the ability to get other people to help them do their job. Such positions bridge the gap between purely paperwork assignments and the actual production line. They require a high degree of intelligence and the ability and willingness to make decisions. Such jobs are, by no means, limited to the automotive field, and a man trained for such work can usually find a spot in any organization producing an assembly-line product.

Purchasing

The production control man depends upon the purchasing department for his parts and materials, and the purchasing man depends, in turn, on a host of suppliers outside the company for the myriad components that make up the modern automobile. Not only must the buyer in the purchasing department secure gaskets, nuts, bolts, radios, spark plugs, springs, and paint; he must also purchase machine tools, lighting fixtures, office equipment, and other supplies required to tool, operate, and maintain his factory. To do this job intelligently, the buyer needs an almost encyclopedic knowledge of just about everything.

Within a large purchasing department, often employing hundreds of people, specialization is a necessity. It is not unusual to have a man assigned exclusively to purchasing a single item. Such specialization by an individual can mean the end of advancement. A man can become so proficient in the purchase of that one item that he becomes invaluable to the company. This is a career pitfall that should and can be avoided.

The buyer makes his purchases from salesmen, from automotive component manufacturers, and from sales representatives who sell the products of several noncompeting manufacturers. This specialized selling of a specialized product to a limited number of customers is about as far removed from the usual concept of "sales" as it is possible to get. The men engaged in this activity have a deep and comprehensive knowledge of the automobile industry. Quite often they are technically expert in the products that they are selling. Their assignment goes far beyond that of simply filling out an order blank. They must be ready to help the buyer solve the problems posed by the company's engineering and industrial design staffs. Often they are representing a firm with its own research and engineering staff, in which case it is the salesman's task to convince an auto manufacturer that his company's new and improved carburetor, or brake lining should be used on the next model. If, in a given year, over a million and a half Chevrolets are sold, the incorporation of a given brand of brake lining on that model Chevrolet is big business indeed.

Another vital function of the purchasing department is to develop data for production control and factory planning that can be used to make decisions on whether to purchase a component from an outside supplier or whether to manufacture that component in its own factory. Such decisions cannot be made solely on cost figures. They involve a multitude of factors, including labor supply, available machinery within the plant, production schedules for other components, availability of raw materials, and factory floor space. The men who must make these decisions may be specialists in one phase of the plant's operation, but in deciding to buy or manufacture a specific component, this specialization must be augmented by a thorough understanding of all phases of the factory's operation.

Assembly

The market has been researched, the automobile has been engineered and styled, the design has been production engineered, and the assembly line has been laid out and balanced by the industrial engineering department. The parts have been purchased, and production control has scheduled the flow of materials. By now it would appear that the actual "making" of the automobile is but an anticlimax. And this is almost literally true.

This is not to say that the manufacture of a modern automobile is a simple matter. It is not. It is simply that the specialization that has taken place within the automobile industry is such that the actual assembly of the car has become but a single operation in a long and complicated process.

The completed automobile is the product of a coordinated team of specialists, and at every stage of its manufacture, from the prefabrication of small parts to the completed automobile, each operation is checked by additional specialists from quality control and inspection.

Before the bright and shiny new hardtop rolls out of the factory gate, many more specialists will have contributed their talents to the final product.

Personnel

In these days of strong automotive unions, the personnel man plays an increasingly important roll in the total operation of the plant. With many labor policies rigidly prescribed by union contract, a mistake in employee policies could result in a strike that might cause a manufacturer to lose his competitive position in the national market. No longer does the personnel department simply hire and fire; it is vitally concerned with every operation in the plant.

Accounting and Fiscal Control

In an operation as complex as that of manufacturing an automobile, the accounting and fiscal control sections become of vital importance. Unless tight control is maintained over all of the costs incurred in the production, the price charged the customer becomes a matter of guesswork. No businessman will long tolerate guessing in the profit and loss statement. Within most corporations, the controller exercises substantial power, and the automobile companies are no exceptions.

In 1955, the value of the passenger cars produced by the auto industry was put at almost $10,000,000,000. Although most of the automotive manufacturers are in strong financial condition, none of them can finance all of the many facets of their business entirely out of cash on hand. The banking business is intimately linked with the automotive world, from the purchase of large stocks of raw material right down to the installment credit issued to the ultimate individual who purchases the finished car.

Expansion, in the form of new assembly plants or specialized component manufacturing installations, is financed out of the sale of stock to the public. It is usually the controller who oversees these varied and often devious fiscal operations, without which his corporation would be unable to function.

Law

This still does not exhaust the list of skills required by the automotive industry. One out of six patents filed at the U. S. Patent Office is in the automotive field—hence the need for patent lawyers. Tax lawyers, corporation law experts, and real property lawyers will also be found on the staff.

Traffic Control

The entire range of maintenance skills—power plant engineers, electricians, plumbers, carpenters and janitors, safety engineers and plant guards, doctors and nurses, recreation supervisors and training directors—are all required. The list is endless, and there has been no attempt to list the skills required of the workers in the factory itself.

The automobile has created our vast network of highways, and it uses these highways—plus the railroads and the sea lanes—to coordinate its far flung network of factories. Ford assembles its automobiles on both the east and west coasts in addition to turning out thousands of Fairlanes and Thunderbirds at the famed River Rouge installation in Detroit. Components for these assembly plants are produced at Rouge and at component supply plants all over the country. These parts must be shipped to the assembly points with precise timing in order to keep the assembly lines humming. Freight traffic control is another one of those vital, though unseen, specialties required in the production of the American automobile.

Advertising, Public Relations, and Sales

But all of this vast organization is useless unless the end product —the finished automobile—can be sold to the consumer. And to accomplish this end, the automobile companies have developed vast advertising, public relations, and sales organizations that literally reach into every home in the country.

Through newspapers, billboards, radio, magazines, and television, the auto manufacturer exploits every phase of the hard sell and the soft sell to convince the public that they should drive his particular make of car. Much of this feverish promotion is prepared by an advertising agency, hired by the manufacturer, to beat the drums for his model. But, even within the company itself, big advertising departments exist in order to keep the hoopla about the company's car constantly before the public. Ford publishes a magazine for all Ford owners that utilizes name writers and artists and is far superior to many newsstand efforts. General Motors has a carnival on wheels that tours the country giving shows extolling the wonders of science and the wonders of General Motors automobiles.

Artists, photographers, entertainers, masters of ceremony, and carnival barkers all find a place in the promotion departments of the big motor manufacturers. But the sales effort does not stop at advertising. Factory representatives travel the country helping dealers to solve their problems and making suggestions on how the dealer can sell more and more cars. Customer complaints must be satisfied, and a department exists to see that a Plymouth customer remains a happy Plymouth customer.

To keep a customer happy, the dealer must furnish good service. To make this possible, the factories run courses in special training centers to teach mechanics how to solve the ills that develop in any car and, in particular, how to solve the problems in their new model.

The sales department of an auto manufacturer must make its sales through the independent, local businessman who owns his own automobile agency. To keep these men happy, the manufacturer sponsors sales contests that send the winners to Hawaii or Bermuda, stage regional sales conventions and meetings, prepare mail order salesmen's training courses, provide information on financing and insurance plans, help run public automobile shows, cooperate with local automobile clubs, and—in general—do everything conceivable to assist their dealers to sell more cars.

Once the automobile is sold to a customer, the factory's role in its product is diminished, but it is by no means finished. Spare parts have to be provided, and the owner must be supplied with a continual stream of information about the fine automobile he has just purchased. People purchase a new car every few years and the factory wants to make certain that the next purchase is the same make as the first.

Insurance

But, the factory is only the prime mover in the complex of businesses that make up the total automotive picture. Auto insurance alone, for example, is a $4½ billion a year business. Installment credit in 1955, a peak automotive year, was $15½ billion, and in such routine items as wax and cleaners for automobiles, the total annual volume was almost $50 million.

State governments in 1955 built 52,000 miles of roads and now the federal government has launched a gigantic road building program. The list can go on and on—gas stations, tire stores, independent garages, car rental services, retail auto supply stores, glass replacement shops, parking lots, quick car-washes, and more remote operations, such as motels and drive-in movies.

Pitfalls and Opportunities

This then, is the automobile industry.

But how does the description of such an industry—one that offers

within the corporation are likely to be a few plants or offices that, while requiring the services of a personnel man, make only routine demands on him. Perhaps the people who work in these offices are either professional or clerical personnel. In a situation such as this, a personnel man has only to solve the regular problems of hiring and firing, taking care of group insurance and pension plans, and listening to the woes of the supervisors and employees. The man handling these routine problems is much less likely to attract the attention of the central corporation office than is the man in a plant who has the job of solving delicate labor union disputes—disputes that could lead to expensive work stoppages and strikes.

Chemists are used throughout the auto industry. However, at an assembly plant, this specialist's duties may be limited to running tests on the paint mixtures used to spray the completed car. At the central research center of the corporation, this same chemist may be at work on more basic and far more interesting development projects.

Within the smaller divisions of a corporation, there are many demands for "one of a kind" specialists. The young man who finds himself in such a position has two courses of action open to him if he desires advancement within the corporation. He may devise new work for himself within his specialty and hope that his initiative and inventiveness will call attention to his ability and thus gain him a more responsible post elsewhere in the corporation. Or, he can try to learn a great deal about the other phases of his local operation and seek promotion to an administrative job within his own plant. In this second case, it means the early abandonment of his speciality.

"One of a kind jobs" are not without their advantages. Usually they provide far more latitude for a variety of experience than a similar specialized position within a large department. Here, the personality of the young man seeking a career should be the deciding factor in the choice. In either case, it is important for the young man to realize that these differences do exist and that the decision to work for a given division of a corporation is just as important as the original decision to go to work for the corporation.

The young man starting a career in industry must really solve two separate and seemingly contradictory problems. He must become expert in his chosen speciality, and, at the same time, he must develop a feel for all of the other specialities that are required within his corporation. In the auto industry, this range of specialities is very large indeed.

How can this be done?

How can a young man learn all of the many things that he must learn about his assignment in the purchasing department and, at the same time, acquire knowledge about areas as diverse as personnel and engineering? Admittedly, this is not easy. It requires an admission on the part of the young man that he really can never learn too much about the world around him, and it requires that he take a sympathetic and an understanding view of the problems faced by departments other than his own.

This need for a broad, understanding approach to the many facets of a company's operation is one of the reasons why the A.B. graduate often performs so well—in the long run—in the business world. While not specifically equipped to do a specialized job at the time he graduates from college, his training is such that he is able to analyze the total problems of the corporation with perspective.

Highly specialized industrial operations, such as those devoted entirely to research and development problems, are experiencing considerable difficulty in obtaining administrative personnel from within their own engineering ranks. It is not enough for a man to be a fine engineer. He must also be able to view the total problems of his company clearly.

All of this is by way of saying that no young man's education can be considered finished at commencement. As the word implies, this is only the beginning.

It is hoped that this chapter has made clear the two problems that face the young man in search of a career.

1. The young man must early choose a specific occupational area.

2. He must give considerable thought to the kind of industry that he will enter in order to put his specific interests to best advantage.

The following chapters of the book will treat both of these problems in more detail.

CHAPTER THREE

TEST TUBES, SLIDE RULES AND DRAFTING TABLES

THE ADVERTISEMENTS in the daily papers look wonderful—and those in the Sunday editions look even better. Lockheed in Atlanta is looking for electronic engineers at $15,000 a year. Boeing in Seattle wants mechanical engineers starting at $12,000. Martin, in Baltimore, will pay between $5,000 and $6,000 to young engineers just out of college. Western Electric and Bell Laboratories are looking for scientists at top salaries. The future for the technical man looks bright indeed in the years ahead.

And the proof of the great future that lies ahead for the technical man is not limited to the advertising columns. The editorial pages of the same daily newspapers decry the fact that Russia is training technical men at a pace faster than are the schools of the United States. The future fate of the nation is said to rest in the hands of the next generation of scientists and engineers.

The implication of all this is that the young man in search of a career need only obtain an engineering diploma from a college— any college—and his future is assured.

Even in the most hectic days of the scramble for engineering talent, this situation never existed. And current trends in the industrial world indicate that the engineer will have to work just as hard for advancement to a top administrative post as will college graduates in other fields.

However, due to the great publicity that has been showered on the general subject of science, vast numbers of young men have crowded the technical courses of the nation's colleges. The result of this rush to the slide rule has been an abundance of good talent concentrated in one single field. This concentration of good talent in the technical field means two things. It means that while competition for the top jobs within engineering is very keen, companies are competing with each other for the better graduates leaving the colleges each year.

What kind of technical personnel is industry seeking?

To man their research, development, and product engineering sections, industry needs three separate and distinct types of people. Let us consider them one at a time.

The Scientist

Many industrial organizations play fast and loose with the term "research." The definition may range all the way from an investigation of basic phenomena to the search for a new way to weld a handle on a frying pan. In the first case, "research" is the correct term. In the second instance, "product engineering" is the proper term.

Actually, there is very little real "research" under way in industry. It has only been very recently that industry has awakened to the fact that "finding out why the grass is green" is important. Now, some of the big electronic and aircraft manufacturers are slowly building research staffs. Only a few of the big corporations—such as Bell Laboratories, Standard Oil of New Jersey, and duPont— have a history of supporting studies into basic physical and chemical problems, the solutions of which promised no immediate gain for the stockholders.

The college recruiter who casually mentions his firm's "research" department should be questioned closely by the college senior to determine in just what sense the word is used. If the young man is seriously interested in pure research, he will be most unhappy in a product engineering section, even though the word "research" is painted on the office door.

Now, as in the past, the great bulk of the pure research being carried out in this country is being done on the college campus. But now, unlike the past, the campus research laboratory is being subsidized by industry and by government or foundations. Now the college professor is quite likely to earn extra money for his research and is likely to be supplied with excellent equipment with which to work out his experiments.

Pure research is usually carried out on the campus. Large laboratories, such as the Applied Physics Laboratory of Johns Hopkins, the Lincoln Laboratory of the Massachusetts Institute of Technology, and the Cornell Aeronautical Laboratory, are actually product development centers at work on specific engineering problems largely of governmental origin. While the caliber of such operations is high, there is little pure research under way.

The young man with a burning desire to explore the unknown areas of science makes a number of decisions simultaneously with his original decision to enter research work. He virtually shuts himself off from high industrial administrative posts. He commits himself to advanced academic studies—the Ph.D. is fast becoming the prerequisite for pure research. He places himself in a position where he will be able to make a most attractive, although not spectacular, salary. And, perhaps most important of all, he chooses a field where the personal satisfactions are great.

The young man who selects research work as a lifetime career is also assured that the demand for his services can only increase. The results of pure research are the raw material from which is extracted our growing technology. And it is this growing technology that is the basis for our civilization. America, as a nation, has reached the point in its development where it fully recognizes the importance of insuring that the raw material supply is constantly replaced. The pure research man is literally the key to the future of the nation.

The Development Engineer

In industry the term "research" is often applied to the development engineer. It is this man's job to take the raw material of basic data discovered by the pure research man and to discover just how this data can be applied to a specific piece of equipment which will perform a useful service.

For example, the development engineer may start with the premise that cosmic ray clouds in outer space are capable of reflecting electromagnetic energy. His assignment may be to take this basic bit of information and to design radio equipment which will take advantage of this knowledge in order to guide intercontinental missiles.

In a very real sense this is creative engineering work at its best. It requires a man with a full grounding in basic science and a knack for developing "hardware," as the physical product of engineering is termed. When the college recruiter talks about "research," this is usually the type of work he is describing.

The future for the development engineer is indeed very bright. In aircraft, in electronics, and in nucleonics the basic research people are developing raw data faster than the development engineers can absorb it. The discoveries of the International Geophysical Year have provided information which will keep the development people busy for the next decade.

At the present time, much of the developmental work is in the defense industries. Exceptions are the work in communications being done by International Business Machines and Western Electric in order to take advantage of the "information theory" developed by Bell Laboratories, and the atomic power plants being designed by Westinghouse and others to make use of new discoveries in atomic theory.

Within the nucleonics industry, the mechanical development engineer is about to come back into his own. Long eclipsed by the electronic and the aeronautical engineers, the mechanical engineer will become the key man in atomic engineering. While the theory behind atomic energy is based upon physics, the problems involved in the design of reactors, power generating plants, and even the atomic bomb are primarily mechanical in nature.

The nucleonics industry may not, in the next decade, absorb large quantities of personnel. Governmental security requirements and the general reluctance of private power companies to abandon their present inexpensive power generation plants will limit its growth. However, within the limits of the industry, the engineering positions available are likely to be among the best in developmental engineering.

Once inside industry, the developmental engineer will likely find that his chances of advancing to a top administrative post are far better than those of his colleague in the "pure" research field. American industry has an inbred respect for the man who develops a piece of "hardware" that will do a job. The salary of the man who selects developmental engineering is also apt to be greater than that paid to the "pure" research worker. The ultimate factor for a young man to consider in deciding whether he wishes to become a "pure" research man or a developmental engineer will be whether he prefers (1) to search for the basic truths behind physical phenomena or (2) to design equipment to take advantage of the truths discovered by others. Of necessity it will be a highly personal choice.

The Product Engineer

The product engineer is that breed of engineer most in demand by all segments of industry. It is his job to make a better frying pan, a smaller radio receiver, a more powerful automobile engine, a faster card-sorting machine, or what-have-you. Without him the vast technology upon which the American economy is based would come to a slow, grinding halt.

However, the young man who chooses to enter this area of engineering should survey the field with special care. It is within product engineering that specialization reaches its zenith. If the young man does not wish to be limited to designing better and better IF strips for better and better UHF receivers, he should question the college recruiter closely.

Industry yearly has need of vast numbers of young engineers. The great majority of them are needed simply to solve the daily, routine problems that arise in the design of even the most simple product. Many of these young men will spend the rest of their lives working on these small details. Because of the high starting wages for engineers, the profession has attracted great numbers of intelligent and talented young men. Not all of them can become project leaders, and only disillusionment awaits the young man who feels that he will achieve automatic promotions simply because he is an engineer.

This is a competitive field, and the young man who enters it should be ready to face that competition.

While there are many routine assignments within product engineering, there is also a great deal of satisfaction to be derived from making something new.

The opportunities for engineering personnel to move into higher administrative posts are also good. More and more industries with a technical base are looking for technically minded men to man their sales and administrative departments. Quite often the young engineer will find that the way to advance within the corporation is to leave engineering. However, this is a situation that he must face when and if it arises.

Other Technical Assignments in Industry

In civil engineering, the research, development, and product engineering assignments, of course, do not exist. However, this field is going to be one of the most active of the engineering professions in the next decade. Not only are there going to be great opportunities within the United States, but the overseas demand for trained civil engineers is going to be even greater. The awakening of the underdeveloped countries, coupled with large American foreign aid programs, will provide opportunities for years to come.

Within the chemical industry the young man seeking a career should realize that the better assignments usually go to the research and development man. The chemical engineer is very likely to find himself watching dials and recording readings in a vast automatic chemical plant.

Again, the young man will be well advised to question the college recruiter carefully on the nature of the "engineering" work being offered. There are exciting and interesting jobs for the chemical engineer, and there are dull and unimaginative assignments also. A few questions to the college recruiter may help the young man avoid the latter.

Beginning Assignments in Engineering

The competition between industrial organizations, particularly in the electronics and aircraft industries, has forced the starting salary for young engineers to unheard of heights. These high starting salaries have, in turn, been responsible for the large amounts of publicity that the engineering profession has received. Companies in these industries know that a young man just out of college is not worth $6,000 a year. But this is the going market price, and they must pay that price in order to get their share of the young graduates. For the young man, this is a very happy state of affairs. He gets good wages in his first job. It is only after he has been on the job a few years that the economics of the industry begin to catch up with him. Because of his high starting salary, he quite often finds that he reaches the limit of his earning power in a short time. An engineer working for the same company for ten years may find that he is earning about $9,000. Since he started at almost $6,000, he figures that he has only had a 50 per cent raise. His classmate who started for $4,200 in the personnel department ten years ago is also making about $9,000. He has had over a 100 per cent raise.

Assayed in the cold light of logic, the engineer is still in a fine position. His total ten-year income is greater than that of his friend. But people do not always act in the cold light of logic, and this slowly increasing salary scale for engineers is largely responsible for the job-hopping that many engineers engage in during the first decade or two out of college.

A young man with five years experience as an engineer with company X may find that he is trapped by the company's salary schedule. While the starting salary offered to recent graduates has been regularly increased to meet the demands of the market, similar readjustments in the salary schedule for men with five or six years of experience have not been made. In an attempt to better his earnings, the experienced engineer will switch to company Y simply because company Y puts him into a different salary scale and gives him the opportunity to earn more money.

But what happens to the young man who goes to work for the big corporation as an engineer? After he has had his twenty-minute interview and later has reported to the company's offices for work, what is expected of him?

If, for example, the young man reports to an electronics company, he may be assigned to a section which is working on long-range radar equipment. His first assignment may consist of recording the results of heat runs and of laying out on a drafting table the most efficient method of placing tubes on a small chassis. He will become part of a four- or five-man team working on one small section of a radar transmitter. His group is part of a section at work on the total radar set. This section, in turn, is part of a big department of a hundred or more engineers at work on an integrated radar system.

Every six months he may be evaluated by his group leader and the department head, and he will be given a small raise or a large raise depending upon the evaluation of his work by these men.

After four or five raises, he will find that he is making $7,000 or $7,500 and that he is at the limit of his salary bracket.

It is at this point that the great log jam in engineering jobs occurs. Quite naturally, the young man expects to be promoted into the next salary bracket, but the company may not be able to do this for a number of reasons. First, the man's work does not qualify him for a promotion. This is a valid reason for the company to refuse a promotion, but it is one seldom accepted by the employee. Second, there may be no economic justification for the company to promote more men into the next salary bracket. This situation occurs quite often. In order for all of the young engineers hired by a company each year to advance periodically to higher positions within the company, it is necessary for the company to constantly increase its volume of work on hand. For many years, this situation prevailed, and the engineers who entered the profession in the five-year period from 1951 to 1956 moved along from one position to another with the neat precision of an assembly line.

There is reason to believe that a similar period of engineering expansion is not to be expected again short of total war.

A third factor affecting the advancement of young engineers is the nature of the defense industry. In the airframe industry, for example, it is not unusual for three aircraft companies to be building prototypes of a new fighter plane. This requires three separate staffs of engineers at all levels. However, only one production contract will be awarded as the result of tests of the three prototypes. This means that the one company which receives the production contract will continue to have an abundance of engineering jobs, whereas the two losers will be faced with an over-supply of skilled men. Naturally, advancement will be slower in the two less-fortunate companies.

To the individual engineer who feels that he has done an excellent job in the design of a rudder control for a plane that is not going to be built, the failure to gain advancement can cause great bitterness. This bitterness is accentuated by his knowledge that his situation is dictated by the nature of the defense business and has little, if anything, to do with the activity of his company or even his own ability. To improve himself, he must look for a job with another company—either the one which did get the production contract or one which is busily at work on a prototype of a bomber.

Still another factor which often thwarts the young engineer in his search for a better job is the stockpiling of junior engineers by a company in the hope that a contract will be obtained to enable the company to make use of these men. It is impossible for a young man, at the time of his college interview, to know if he is being stockpiled. And, should the company's hopes fail to materialize, he will find that he must remain on the drafting board for several years. Since this measure has proven most expensive to industry, it is dying out as a regular practice.

One factor, however, does work in the young engineer's favor. Because of the expense of recruiting and training a young engineer, a company is reluctant to lay him off, even in the event a contract is lost. Engineers are laid off by industry, but they usually enjoy more job security than any other job classification within a company.

As in any line of specialization, there are a limited number of excellent, well-paying jobs in contrast to the much larger number of not so good, not so well-paying jobs. Engineering is exceptional in that even the low-paying jobs offer salaries at a scale above other occupations at similar levels. It is this "floor" under the engineer's salary scale that has made the engineering profession seem to be the cornucopia which it really is not. The top engineer who moves on to a responsible position within any company is a superior man with a number of traits that transcend those of engineering.

Preparation for an Engineering Career

It is unfortunate that most engineering schools do not find time to teach more of the English language. It is the ability to communicate his ideas, more than anything else, that marks an engineer for promotion. It is assumed, of course, that he is a competent engineer. But no matter how competent he is, if he cannot communicate his ideas through reports or in discussions with his department chief or in meetings with production and sales personnel, he will never move very far away from the test bench and the drafting tables. An engineering department head must daily explain the problems of his sections to management and to the sales department. He must write an unending stream of reports on both technical and administrative subjects. In choosing his electives in college, the wisest choice that an engineering student can make in his junior and senior years would be a course in report writing.

Should the student have chosen engineering as an escape from courses that required term papers, he is at a severe disadvantage. The importance of reports within an engineering organization is such that many firms are now hiring young men with A.B. degrees to train as administrative engineers. These administrators must have a flair, if not formal training, for engineering, and it is their job to interpret the work of their sections to management and to other departments within the plant. The slide rule has not yet completely replaced the written word. Similar jobs within engineering organizations are available for A.B. graduates in the technical writing field. At the present time, the salary scales for technical writers are below those of engineers, but the importance of the work is becoming more widely recognized and this gap is slowly being closed.

Perhaps in no other field, outside of education, is the advanced degree held in such esteem as it is in engineering. One of the reasons for this is the tendency of government agencies to judge the ability of a company to do a specific job on the basis of the educational background of its personnel. The M.A. and the Ph.D. have direct monetary value in engineering. When weighing his decision to accept a job with a company, the engineer should determine what opportunities exist in the area to enable him to continue his studies. And, once started upon such a course of study, it is important that he finish it. There are, of course, old timers in every organization who have come up the hard way without degrees. But, as a whole, engineers today are college graduates and are academically oriented. The attainment of an advanced degree can be one way of breaking the log jam that every engineer comes in contact with three to five years after leaving school.

Most young men are attracted toward engineering because they have a healthy interest in the world around them and a real desire to make new things which will do a new and better job. For these men, engineering itself is reward enough. The monetary considerations, while important, are actually secondary to their desire to do the thing that they most want to do.

However, the word "engineering" has been much overused, and it is a good idea to know just what is involved in the term "engineering" as interpreted by industry.

A lot of things have been called engineering such as sales. But the tacking on of the word "engineer" neither adds nor detracts from the work of the salesman—it only confuses.

The terms "production engineer" and "industrial engineer" are frequently used. These describe functions that are closely allied with the manufacturing process. The opportunities in this field are covered in the next chapter.

CHAPTER FOUR

PRODUCTION IS THE KEY

THE GREAT boast of America in the past century has been its tremendous production facilities. In war, American industry has filled the sky with planes, the seas with ships, and the land with tanks, trucks, and jeeps. In peace, this same industry has filled the highways with automobiles and the home with television receivers, automatic washers, and power lawn mowers.

The assembly line is the mark of modern American industry, and it is something that is avidly copied by every nation in the world. It is the one American export that meets absolutely no sales resistance—even in the Iron Curtain countries.

When Eli Whitney introduced the principle of interchangeable parts to the manufacture of muskets in the years just before 1800, he began a movement that was to change the face of all America. Mass production greatly diminished the value of the individual craftsman and, in his place, set up a hierarchy of foremen, planners, and administrators whose function it was to direct the activities of large numbers of relatively unskilled workers.

A little over a century later, Henry Ford adapted Whitney's theories to the manufacture of automobiles on a scale that staggered the imagination. Hundreds of thousands of model "T" Fords were produced each year through the combined efforts of production engineers, industrial engineers, production control personnel, quality control teams, and a whole host of supporting clerical and administrative people.

Henry Ford's assembly line techniques have been copied by every

American industry from ball-point pens to the war-time production of flying fortresses. American industry has become marvelously adept at turning out vast numbers of anything for which there is a consumer demand.

American industry has been production-minded. And, because of this, the vast majority of industrial leadership has, in the past, usually come from the various production departments. This is not as true today as it was fifteen or twenty years ago. Industry is now finding top executives in sales, marketing, advertising, fiscal, and legal departments. The road to the top is no longer a single track through the machine shop. However, almost half of all the top executives in the country today received their early training in the production field.

But top executive posts do not tell the entire story. The size and scope of American industry make provision for great numbers of middle management positions in production areas.

For each department, such as industrial engineering, there must be a department chief. In the larger factories this can be a responsible position indeed. The salary for such men, while not in the 80 per cent tax bracket, is large enough to make the job coveted by any ambitious young man.

Wage Scales and Advancement

At this point a word is in order about the wage scales of American industry. There is no such thing as a going rate for an industrial engineer. In industries where the over-all level of pay for factory workers is high—airframe, automobile, electronics—an industrial engineer is likely to earn more than his counterpart in an industry where the general wage scale is low.

Geographic considerations also affect the salaries paid to men in middle management positions. The recent migration of industry to the southern states has been induced by the fact that wages in that area are generally less than those in the more highly industrialized northern sections of the country.

Since the young man in college who is studying to become an industrial engineer is not a specialist in any one industry at the time of his graduation, his first industrial choice is an important one. It is just as easy to become a good industrial engineer in a well-paying industry as it is to become a good industrial engineer in one which pays not quite so well.

The college senior going in for his twenty-minute interview should first check the wage scales of the industry represented by the recruiter in order to be in a position to evaluate any offer that might be made.

At the present time, the industrial scene is in a state of flux brought about by the introduction of automation techniques. Just as Whitney and Ford revolutionized the industrial process, automation is now bringing about what some people are calling "the Second Industrial Revolution." Few people are certain as to what this will mean to the American scene or the American economy over the long pull. But for the individual seeking a place in one of the production phases of industry, the meaning is clear. When such techniques as information theory, programming, and fully automated assembly lines come into common usage, industry's demand for trained personnel will become greater.

The application of these abstract ideas to general production methods will make it more difficult for the man in the shop to rise through the ranks to a supervisory post. The skills learned in the maintenance or operation of automatic equipment are likely to be far different from those required in planning the use of this same equipment.

Traditionally, it has been possible for a worker, through hard work and the demonstration of his abilities, to become an assistant foreman and, later, foreman. As automation techniques transform the administration of a production department into more abstract paperwork channels, the need for the traditional foreman will gradually disappear.

The trend has only begun. Many foremen are still coming out of the production groups. But one large company has already announced that it will, for the next five years, fill all vacancies in its production supervision ranks with A.B. graduates.

It is interesting to note that A.B. men are being sought for these positions. It is felt that men with some background in psychology, sociology, and economics will be well qualified for these supervisory posts. As the direction of a production department involves more and more the handling of people and the inter-relation of company and labor union, and less and less the instruction of workers in specific mechanical skills, an entirely new type of production supervisor will be required.

But this trend is still some time off in the future. Of more immediate concern to the young man about to graduate from college are those sections of production that are presently requiring college training of the young men entering the ranks.

At the present time, many industrial concerns are looking for college men to fill vacancies in their production engineering, industrial engineering, quality control, and production control sections. This is not a universal rule. While industrial engineering and production engineering have reached the status where the degree is the expected set of credentials for the young applicant, workers from the shop are still being recruited for these positions. The number of night courses in the catalogs of the large urban colleges and universities indicates that many men without a full college background aspire to these jobs. The number of courses also indicates that the college-trained man has a decided advantage over the untrained man. In twenty years, it is estimated that almost half of the working population will have this college background. When that time comes, industry will have no trouble in finding men to fill all of its production supervision and staff positions with men from college ranks. In the meantime, industry will demand the college degree more emphatically each year as the supply of trained men becomes more plentiful.

In quality control and production control sections of industry, the degree requirement is far from universal. But the men who do enter these fields—quality control especially—are likely to be older men with years of factory experience behind them. In quality control sections, a young man needs a degree for entrance to the field. In production control, the degree requirement is becoming mandatory in industries in the process of adapting automation techniques. In the less progressive industries, or in industries where automation is not yet possible, the production control people are not as likely to be recruited from college ranks.

What can the young man expect to find in industry after graduation? What is he likely to be asked to do?

If he is lucky, he may find a corporation that has a production trainee program. In such a program he will spend from three to six months in production engineering, the same period in industrial engineering and similar periods in production and quality control. From his experience in these various departments, he will be able to find out what he likes to do and what he is best able to do. Then, with the help of his supervisors, he will be permanently assigned to one of these four areas.

But such training programs are not numerous enough to accommodate all of the young men from each year's graduation class. Many will have to make their decision at the time of the fateful twenty-minute interview.

Industrial Engineering

The industrial engineer will likely find that his first assignment involves a stop watch and a clip board. His assignment will be to set the rate of a given operation in the plant. This work, of a seemingly routine nature, is of real dollar and cents value to the company. The practice of incentive pay to workers who produce at better than the established time rate for a given operation is widespread, and a mistake on the part of the new industrial engineer will either cost the company money in excess wages paid or bring down upon his head the wrath of the union stewards who believe that he is being unfair to the workers.

As the work of the industrial engineer progresses, he will find that his work involving recommended changes of procedure or of method will quite often bring him into contact with the union. An industrial engineer could put the electives of his senior year to no better use than to use them for labor relations courses.

From the setting of rates, the industrial engineer will move on to problems involving the development of new methods of manufacture, new processes, and the establishment of actual assembly lines. Here he will find that his routine work as a beginner is invaluable to him in the complicated procedure of balancing a line.

A generation ago, when most industrial engineers were recruited from the shop, these men knew what a milling machine was and what could be expected of a planer and an automatic screw machine. The young man from the college campus, unless he has spent his summers working in a machine shop—a good idea for the prospective industrial engineer—will have to learn what these machines will do. Even to plan a fully automatic operation, the industrial engineer must have some idea of the capacity of the machines that he is automating.

These are things that are not learned in any classroom. They must be learned from skilled workers in the shop who have spent the better part of a lifetime learning their trade. Getting to know these men and learning the important things that they have to teach a beginner is an important phase of the young industrial engineer's training.

Advancement will come in the form of salary increases or to the post of assistant chief industrial engineer or chief industrial engineer.

Any further movement must be into the higher posts of management or to a staff position. In both cases, the industrial engineer actually leaves his profession behind. Like the electronics engineer who moves into administration and, thereby, leaves behind his slide rule and oscilloscope, the industrial engineer, in making a similar move, leaves behind his stopwatch and clipboard.

Production Engineering

There is a great deal of lateral movement in industry between the production engineering sections and the industrial engineering groups. In smaller companies, the two types of work may be combined in a single department.

Production engineering is the first stage of the manufacturing process. It is at this point that the new product, developed by engineering design sections, is first considered from a manufacturing standpoint. To be considered are such factors as the over-all capacity of the plant, the current backlog of work, the available factory floor space, the available machine tools, the amount of new tooling required by the new product, the workload in the tool design section, the available manpower in the plant, and even the available skilled manpower in the general geographic vicinity of the plant. These factors and many more involving delivery dates promised by the sales department, the projected sales price of the product, and the availability of raw materials must all be studied by the members of the production engineering group before the product can be released to production.

In many respects the functions of production engineering groups are staff functions. The decisions of the group are prepared in the form of a report and passed on to higher management for study and for action.

The plant may go on two shifts in order to meet a schedule. It may subcontract the necessary tooling. It may manufacture some of the detail parts of the product rather than wait for delivery from an outside supplier. These are important decisions, and they are decisions that are arrived at only after a long study and a thorough evaluation of all of the many factors involved.

Industry has great need of college trained personnel in production engineering. It is assumed that the young man who has spent four years in college will have learned how to make this type of thorough study and that he will have learned how to make decisions on the basis of the data that he has gathered.

However, the young man entering a production engineering section should not assume that he will begin immediately to make earth-shaking or even factory-shaking decisions. His first task and his subsequent assignments for the first year or two of his working life will be spent in tracking down information and compiling lists of facts and statistics that are to be used by his seniors in solving the problems at hand.

Such assignments will seem dull and repetitive. At times, it will be very frustrating when his hard work of several days or a week is tossed aside and never used because someone further up the line has decided that the problem should be attacked from an entirely new angle.

Advancement, as in the case of the industrial engineer, will come in the form of salary increases or in promotion to a staff position or to the post of assistant chief production engineer or to chief production engineer.

At this point, it should be pointed out that the higher management production posts, such as assistant factory manager or factory manager, are often made from among the four men who head up the four production groups of industrial engineering, production engineering, production control, and quality control. Men who have advanced to these responsible positions are usually considered by management to have proven themselves to have superior ability. The choice for more responsible jobs is then made on the basis of personality or even personal preference. It is only natural for a factory manager to choose a man he knows well; a man he likes and trusts as his assistant.

But to return to the prospective production engineer. The college training of a young man seeking a career in this field is likely to be very similar to that of the industrial engineer. He will have had courses in time and motion study, industrial organization, labor relations, and industrial management.

However, once inside a particular plant, he is likely to discover that its methods of operation are quite different from the examples of factory operation he read about in his textbooks. The segment of his college training that is likely to be the most use to him is the method of attacking new problems that his professors in every course, from freshman English to advanced labor relations, tried to instill in him.

Because of the importance of this training to the production engineer, there is little reason why liberal arts students from the English, history, or philosophy departments cannot become good production engineers. Convincing the recruiter that this is the case, however, may be a formidable job. The age of specialization is truly with us, and it has caused the requirements for specific jobs to be rigidly prescribed. This is an unfortunate state of affairs that is not likely to be changed in a twenty-minute interview—no matter how persuasive the student may be.

Quality Control

There are two separate and distinct phases to quality control. The first is inspection. Men are normally recruited for these positions from the shop, and they are men wise in the ways of their fellow workers. They know what can be done with a lathe, a milling machine, or a radial drill, and they know what is expected by management in the way of quality work. This is experience that can be gained only in the shop, and the college-trained man must spend years in getting this type of knowledge before he will be the equal of the shop trained inspector.

The second phase of quality control work is more abstract. It is both analytical and statistical. It consists of discovering how fast an assembly line can be run before the number of rejected units outweighs the gain in production obtained by the speed-up. It consists of discovering the required sampling of units that must be inspected in the incoming inspection section of the department in order to ascertain that the standard of a given lot of detail parts from a supplier is of sufficient quality to enable that lot to be released for use on the production lines. It consists of devising simple, though positive, methods of checking the products made in the plant. In this respect, the work is similar to that of the industrial engineer.

The job of the quality control man often makes severe demands upon his self-control. No production supervisor and, for that matter, no worker likes to be told that he is doing inferior work. Yet it is the task of the quality control man to discover just when and where poor work is being done. Sharp differences of opinion are likely to arise between the quality control man and the people in production. Tact in dealing with people and the ability to make people see that his point of view is the correct one are essential to the young man who decides to go into this phase of industrial work.

The man who is afraid of being disliked will be at a disadvantage. He will always be tempted to relax his standards in order to gain the approval of his fellow workers. Such an attitude is fatal in a quality control man.

Advancement for a man in the quality control department will be similar to that of the production engineer or the industrial engineer.

The training in college for the quality control man will also be similar to that of these two groups. However, a heavy dose of statistics should be added to the curriculum. Quality control work is becoming more and more statistical and theoretical in nature. This trend can only continue as the human factor is gradually eliminated from the production process by automation techniques.

In the routine industrial production situation, the quality control man is simply another department in the chain of departments that makes up the total industrial scene. However, in more precision industries, such as that segment of the airframe industry devoted to large missiles, the quality control man becomes one of the key figures in the operation. The number of missile firing failures at Cape Canaveral graphically points up the importance of quality control in a situation where total inspection is required. With literally a million dollars at stake on every firing, the responsibility of the inspector and the quality control man is indeed great.

Production Control

Production control is one phase in industrial production that is going to see the most sweeping changes as automation techniques come into general usage. Traditionally, production control sections have been staffed by promoting men from the shop, first to expediter and then to more responsible positions as they demonstrate their ability to handle them.

The job itself calls for great attention to detail and, in many respects, is quite demanding. Production control is the department charged with seeing that the right number of detail parts and subassemblies reach the proper spot on the assembly line at the proper time. The rage of an assembly line foreman who is forced to slow or stop his line because some error has prevented the arrival of the materials that he needs is something to behold. And the displeasure of the foreman is reflected in a more refined but just as positive manner by all of management right up to the factory manager.

The production control section comes into contact with almost every segment of the industrial organization. It must work with purchasing, with the detail manufacturing sections, with inventory control, with the material moving groups, with production engineering, and with the final production departments themselves. When one of these groups falls behind in the scheduling required for the production of a given product, it is the task of the production control section to take action to bring the schedule back in line. It is a task that requires tact, initiative, diplomacy, and a high degree of common sense. It is no place for the man who becomes rattled easily or who does not like to work under pressure.

Within recent years there has been a trend within industry to recruit college-trained men to fill positions in production control. This has been brought about, in part, by the introduction of automatic equipment and, in part, by the realization that careful planning by a man capable of evaluating a problem and thinking it through to a firm conclusion could eliminate many of the difficulties normally encountered in production control situations. Further automation and the additional advanced planning that is required by complex automatic machinery will only accentuate this trend.

Advancement in this phase of production work is again similar to that outlined for the three jobs described above.

The college recruiter is likely to be looking for men to fill production control positions from the industrial management and the industrial engineering courses. But the type of man required in production control posts actually has little need to know very much about industry. An A.B. with the personality and the initiative to tackle a complex organizational problem is equally as capable of handling such an assignment as a man from the more specialized courses. Some concerns do hire A.B.'s for this type of work. Therefore, an A.B. graduate with some interest in entering the production side of industry may not be entirely wasting his time should he sign up for a twenty-minute interview with a recruiter in search of production control personnel.

While production is of great importance in the total picture of American industry, it is not of equal importance in every company. Some companies are very production minded and consistently move their top production people into the highest management positions. Others place more emphasis on research and development and, therefore, look for leadership in their technical sections. Still others are traditionally sales-minded and, in these companies, the top posts are likely to go to men from sales and marketing departments.

The young man seeking an interview with a recruiter from any company should first attempt to discover where that company places its emphasis. Biographies of top management people in "Who's Who" are one source of information and the advance literature passed out by the college placement bureau often contains this type of information. However, a company's recruiting literature should be carefully evaluated because it is going to present the best possible picture of any operation. If the information cannot be found before the interview, the college senior should put the question squarely to the interviewer. In most cases, he will get an honest answer.

The positions available to college graduates in industry are, of course, not limited to the production departments. Industrial opportunities in personnel, industrial relations, accounting, and purchasing will be covered in Chapter Six.

CHAPTER FIVE

SALES SETS THE PACE

THE YOUNG MAN beginning to cast about for a career in the business world may have his choice influenced by a number of factors. He may want to follow in the footsteps of his father or a succesful older brother. He may have an uncle whom he admires, or he may be influenced by a friendly neighbor. These are personal contacts, and contacts of this nature can provide the young man with first-hand knowledge of a specific career.

But, quite often, these personal contacts are not numerous enough to enable the young man to make up his mind. He then must turn to what he has read and to what he has learned in school and in college and then decide what he wants to do from a study of secondary sources.

Unfortunately for the sales and advertising professions, the secondary sources do not offer much encouragement to the young man seeking information about these fields. In his American literature class, he is taught to sneer at the pretentions of the real estate selling Babbitt; in his drama class he is appalled by Arthur Miller's pathetic figure in *Death of a Salesman;* in his course on "Modern American Thought," he learns that mass advertising has debased American culture, and in his English class he is told that Winstons taste good *as* (not like) a cigarette should.

Both in and out of class, the sales and advertising occupations enjoy a universally bad press. And when the young man contrasts the lurid tales of Madison Avenue with the more inspiring stories of men who became great lawyers, doctors, educators, physicists, engineers, and business leaders, it is little wonder that salesmen and advertising men appear to be miserable, money-grubbing men. Even the ruthless industrial barons of the turn of the century seem to be honest, straightforward cut-throats when compared to the sly, devious men who manipulate the public through shady methods of motivational research.

The result of this steady barrage of propaganda is that young men choose almost any career except that of a salesman. But the nation's businesses need salesmen. And, in the next ten years, it will require them in increasing numbers.

Sales Recruitment

How does business recruit its salesmen at the present time?

It recruits them mainly from within its own ranks. In the technical fields, it is not at all unusual for an engineer with three or four years experience in industry to decide that the sales department offers a great many opportunities. Somehow, once inside the business world, the young man's concept of the salesman undergoes a startling change. The salesman who is working desperately hard to keep orders flowing into the factory in order that the production lines can continue to roll at full capacity no longer appears to be a villain.

Business administration students drift into sales when the glamour of office work has lost its appeal. School teachers become insurance salesmen after a few summers of toying with the idea on a part-time basis, and sociologists and psychologists drift into advertising because there are exciting, demanding, and well-paying jobs in that field.

It is true that many large firms send recruiting teams to the campus each spring, and, by offering the college graduate extensive and valuable training programs, many of these firms are able to secure a goodly number of bright young men to enter their sales and merchandising departments. But, at the same time, many young men with the ability and the personality to make good salesmen and good sales executives choose to enter other careers rather than become a "huckster."

Five or six years later, when the mental picture formed in American literature and drama has dimmed, these same young men drift into sales work and begin their careers. It is just this sort of drifting that this book is designed to prevent. There is no reason why a young man should have to spend several years working in industry before he discovers that "salesman" is not a title that must be borne with shame.

Salesmanship and the American Economy

For any one book to attempt, in a single chapter, to undo the work of Sinclair Lewis, Arthur Miller, and Frederick Wakeman is to attempt the impossible. Nevertheless, below are some of the facts that make salesmanship one of the most important, if not the most important, factors in the present American economy.

At the present time, it is freely admitted that American industry is capable of producing far more goods and services than the American people are able or willing to consume. It is also freely acknowledged that the country is facing a real population explosion. By 1975, it is estimated that there will be 222.3 million people in this country. Unless the nation can be convinced that it must consume more and more goods, we are going to be faced with a serious labor problem. While a total population of 222 million will automatically mean that there will be many more consumers in the marketplace, the advance of automation means that less and less human labor will be required to satisfy their needs.

The leaders of American industry are not unaware of this problem, and they have already formulated several attacks on this threat to our economy. Many of industry's approaches to this problem are through the area of sales and merchandising.

The present high fidelity industry is a perfect case in point. In 1947, the phonograph industry was moribund. Its sales were down and television was about to invade the market in the search for the consumer's dollar. The long playing record was introduced to the mass market. This was not a technical achievement. Radio transcriptions had been played at 33⅓ rpm for years. Concurrently with the introduction of the new records came a great improvement in the home equipment needed to play the new records. Again, this was not a technical improvement. The first few years of high-fidelity equipment manufacture simply introduced to the American market record players based on pre-war English designs. The industry boomed.

The public began to absorb more and more records. Classical music became a part of every home. The price of records went down. The price of the new and better record players went down. And the public created a great new industry. In 1947, few record stores could exist on the sale of records alone. They had to sell radios, refrigerators, musical instruments, and sheet music to make ends meet. Now there are many specialized record stores. Record Clubs that sell by mail are an industry in themselves. And the revolution in the phonograph industry is not over yet.

With the boom in sales, money was poured back into research and now stereo records may replace conventional monaural records, and the cycle that began in 1947 will begin all over again.

The point to be made here is that aggressive sales produced a market. It created a desire where there was no desire. It took the tools that were available and fashioned a new industry. And what was once done for high fidelity can be repeated in hundreds of other industries.

On a less exalted plane, the deodorant phase of the cosmetics industry has carved out a market where none existed before. While making Americans intensely aware of underarm perspiration, advertising men have created a multi-million dollar industry. On a larger scale, the entire cosmetics industry is the prime example of the importance of sales and merchandising techniques in our society. The large cosmetic houses that cater to the fair sex are primarily advertising and sales organizations. It costs far more to advertise a lipstick than it does to make it. And the result is that the production facilities of the cosmetic industry are the least important phase of the total operation. While this is an exception, many other industries are showing a trend in the same direction.

Small appliance manufacturers maintain engineering staffs to look for new ways to improve their products, but it is the sales and merchandising sections that dictate the policies of the business. Appliances have their big years when they manage to convince the housewife that she can no longer keep house without a rotisserie, a deep fryer, or an automatic skillet. None of these products present formidable engineering or production problems. It is the success of the sales department that keeps the factories growing and large numbers of people employed.

The kind of creative selling that has been talked about here is a long way from the hearty, back-slapping caricature of a salesman who is usually pictured by the layman.

But, if sales is not the man in the loud voice, badgering the customer to sign his name on the dotted line, just what is sales?

To answer that question, let us look at one phase of sales and merchandising at a time. Every type of product and, to some extent, every separate product presents different sales problems. Industrial sales problems are entirely different from those of retailing; the food and drug industries pose far different problems than does the appliance industry, and a mail order operation stands in sharp contrast to sales organizations that send their representatives from door to door.

Let us examine these various facets of sales and merchandising in detail.

Sales in Industry

The chapter on the automobile industry touched briefly upon the role of the salesman who specialized in the sale of one product or one type of product to a limited number of customers. In the case of the automobile industry, the salesman's clientele was extremely limited. For that reason, it is probably an atypical case. More representative of industrial sales is the man who sells components in the electronics industry.

The manufacture of the components that go into electronic equipment is a highly specialized business often requiring extensive automatic machinery. For example, only a few of the very largest firms in electronics attempt to manufacture tubes, and almost none of them make their own resistors and capacitors. Such components are the lifeblood of electronics, and are purchased in large numbers by all of the manufacturers of electronic equipment, and the competition for such sales is intense.

A hypothetical salesman for such a components manufacturer may work for a factory with headquarters in Buffalo and cover a territory consisting of Virginia, West Virginia, Delaware, Maryland, and parts of Pennsylvania. He has desk space and a telephone answering service in Washington and a list of over one-hundred customers ranging from large manufacturing plants to small research laboratories. Needless to say, he travels a great deal and sees very little of his family. He works hard, traveling by day and filing reports for the Buffalo office at night in a hotel room. He is paid well and has a generous expense account.

The chances are that he is a college man with a liberal arts, business administration, or engineering degree. He has spent several years working in the Buffalo plant as a sales coordinator or an engineer. He has enough knowledge of the problems of the factory to be able to explain to his customers that delivery cannot be expected yesterday. He reads the trade journals and has a thorough knowledge of his specialty and of the electronics industry as a whole.

In addition to offering the products within his company's line, he may quite often offer the research and engineering facilities of his company in order to solve some particular problem vexing one of his customers.

He is quiet, soft-spoken, and serious. His contacts within the customer's establishment are the members of the purchasing department and, quite often, the engineering department. His technical background is sufficient to enable him to converse with both of these groups with equal ease. Usually his customers are glad to see him. He not only offers products and services that they need, but he is also a source of information about new developments within the components industry and with the electronics industry in general.

He aspires to a sales executive post at the home office and possibly, later, an even more responsible position in management. However, if he is a good salesman, he may find himself in the situation where he is making more money working out of his Washington office than does the vice-president in charge of sales at the home office. Industry, unlike the novelists, fully recognizes the value of the salesman and pays him accordingly.

But the salesman working for the components manufacturer is still on somebody's payroll, and the salesman, long separated from the home office, soon develops independent ways. When this happens, the logical step for the man is into the role of the sales representative. As such, he becomes an independent businessman representing several different product lines in a given geographic area. As a sales representative, he has the same problems that he had as a salesman for a specific manufacturer—multiplied by the number of product lines that he is representing. He now pays his own expenses out of his commissions and works perhaps harder than he did before. If he is fortunate enough to obtain some of the better product lines, his income can be excellent indeed. Incomes of between $25,000 and $50,000 are not impossible for the hard-working sales representative.

The life is not easy, but the rewards are great. It takes a very high post indeed in staff management or the engineering department of a manufacturing concern to equal the income of a top salesman or sales representative. And, as a salesman to industry, he is performing a service vital to that industry.

The Food and Drug Industries

The food and drug industries present almost identical sales and merchandising opportunities and, for that reason, may be considered at the same time. Both have become industries dominated by the large chain operation. The independent grocery and the independent drug store have become the exception instead of the rule, and all trends point to the fact that chain operation is gaining in strength with every passing year.

Concurrently with the growth of the chain-operated retail outlet for food and drugs has come a growth of the giant food processor and drug manufacturer. Small, regional packers and canners still exist, but, year by year, more of them are acquired by the big corporations by way of mergers. Often these small organizations retain their trade names because these names have regional value, but the men who staff the organizations are men who have come up through the rigid training processes of the parent corporation.

The large food merchandisers, such as General Foods and General Mills, are among the most active recruiters on the college campus. In the drug field, McKesson and Robbins recruits heavily. They are looking for bright boys, but they are not after the genius or the grind. While their representative may look at the grades of the young man who comes in to have his twenty-minute interview, he will also look at the student's record in sports and extracurricular activities. The big food merchandisers are looking for the all-American boy. This is not said in any derogatory sense. These corporations have learned through experience that the young man whom they need for their operations must be able to work with all types of people under a variety of circumstances, must be willing to dig in and do a lot of routine work, and must be bright enough to handle more responsible assignments when the time comes for him to move on to bigger assignments.

Many of these big merchandisers offer the young man a training course. This may be a period of between one and two years and will begin with classroom work in the home office. Here the young man will be exposed to the corporation's product line and to its method of operation. After several months of "theory," the young man will be sent on the road. At first, he will be assigned to follow in the footsteps of an old and experienced salesman. Later, he will be on his own. In both cases, the work may seem to be terribly dull and uninteresting. Tacking up signs, setting up displays in drug-store windows, and stocking cans in a neighborhood grocery store or supermarket will begin to seem very far removed from the grand economic theories that the trainee learned as a student.

And the reports to the home office? These are endless. The general pattern is for the young man to be sent first to a rural area where the stores are mainly owned by independent merchants and the distance between stores is great. Gradually, as the training period continues, the trainee is moved to suburban areas and finally to the big city. By this time he has driven more miles than he cares to remember and has stayed at more bad hotels and motels than he can ever forget. Make no mistake, this is not an easy life, but if the young man is still with the company at the end of the training period, he is in line for better things.

While the young man has been on the road, seemingly forsaken by the home office, his performance and his reports have been carefully evaluated. At the end of the training period, he is offered a position in one of two possible areas. He may be assigned to a product area within the central offices of the corporation, or he may be given a group of products to sell within a given geographical location.

Both assignments have advantages and disadvantages. If the company decides that the trainee is destined for product development within the corporation, it is quite possible for the young man to move into a Product Manager's position within the home office at a reasonably early age. It is also possible that the young man will, for a number of reasons, be shunted off into a staff position at the central office where his earning power will be more limited. This is not to be interpreted to mean that the man who ends up in a staff position will starve to death. Such men are very well paid. It is only to state that the real plum within the corporation is the Product Manager's spot and that these men are exceptionally well paid—and that they are usually young men in their thirties of exceptional drive and ability.

Should the young man be assigned to sales work at the end of his training period, he is usually cut off from becoming a Product Manager. But this does not mean that he cannot earn a large salary. Good salesmen in every field are well paid, and the food and drug industries are no exceptions. The appointment to the sales force does mean that it will take a few more years for the man to reach his peak earning power. He still may move into sales supervision at a later date.

All of this would indicate that the young man selected for such a training program simply cannot lose. No matter what happens, according to the possibilities outlined above, the young man is certain to end up in a job that will provide him with an excellent livelihood.

This is all very true. But it is true only for those who finish the training course. And, as we have tried to indicate, the training period is an arduous one. The attrition rate in the corporation training courses is great. Even though no grades are posted and no report cards are handed out, the trainee can usually tell how well he is doing. He also learns very quickly whether or not he is going to like this kind of life as a career.

For this reason, it is well for the young man to learn all that he can about the food and drug industries before he embarks on such a training course. He should also realize that this is the real "basic" training period of his career and that he cannot expect it to be easy. At the beginning the pay is good, but the expenses of traveling and moving from one town to another are high. It is often termed a "single man's game," and the student who get's married at graduation is more likely to have trouble finishing the training grind than is the man who has not yet formed such emotional and financial attachments. But the rewards are high, and the man who "sweats out" the full course is likely to have his career mapped out for him. And it is very likely to be a career that will suit his ability and his talents.

At the other end of the food and drug business is the retail store.

At the present time, the men who rise to managers' positions in these operations are, for the most part, men who have begun as clerks in the store and, through ability and hard work, have reached the top. However, there is reason to believe that, within the next few years, this pattern will change. The reasoning behind this prediction lies in an analysis of the specialized retail chain operation.

The Specialized Retail Chain

To discuss the specialized retail chain operation it is necessary to return to the automobile industry for our examples. Both Goodyear and Firestone conduct extensive college recruiting operations on behalf of their retail outlets. It can, of course, be argued that the Goodyear and Firestone retail outlets are closer to department stores than they are to specialty shops. Yet the fact remains that they are based upon the automotive products produced by the parent companies.

College recruits who enter the programs of these companies are most likely to get a heavy dose of staff operations theory along with some routine training in the retail outlets themselves. At the present time, the volume of young men taken by these companies for training is not large. But it is important because it shows a trend in chain retail operations to insist upon college training before they will accept a man as a candidate for a store managership.

It is only a matter of time before the food and drug industries institute similar programs at the retail level. The drugstore has long been the butt of jokes based upon the variety of products that it sells, and the super-markets, already in the drug, magazine and phonograph record businesses, are invading the field of ready-to-wear clothes and hardware. From here it is only a short step to the department store type of operation.

The Department Store

The department store, particularly one of the size and scope of Macy's or Gimbel's, is the place where retail selling reaches its apex. Combining, under one roof, everything from notions to outboard motors, the department store offers the public the entire range of American consumer goods. Such a sales organization depends upon a variety of offerings to draw a multitude of customers and a volume of sales generated by this hoard of buyers to drive its prices down below that of the thousands of specialty shops that are its competitors throughout a great metropolitan area.

The big chains, such as Sears and J. C. Penny, and the name organizations, such as Macy's, run extensive training programs. Every year these stores comb the college campuses for top notch students to staff their programs. In the department store business both men and women are in demand, and it is one of the few businesses that women can point to and say that the double standard has been, at least in part, ignored.

At Macy's for example, forty or more college graduates enter the training program every year. The training program lasts for one year and consists of a variety of selling and nonselling assignments interspersed with classroom work. At the end of the year's training period, the trainee is judged by a committee of his superiors and is assigned to a staff or to a selling position. Actually the term "selling" is misleading. The trainee sent out into the merchandising end of the business begins as a kind of a staff assistant to the buyer of a department. He then moves, should his ability warrant it, into the positions of assistant buyer, buyer, and merchandise manager.

Should the trainee be tapped for a staff position, his opportunities are still great. An operation the size of Macy's uses all of the functions of personnel, accounting, and stock control which are usually associated with a large corporation.

And at Macy's the trainee's route of advancement may be both through the central organization or through one of the many branch stores. A buyer of a big department in the central store may become a merchandise manager for a branch store, and the supervisor of an accounting department section may become a controller of a store in another city.

The Macy organization has carried the specialization of sales to its ultimate conclusion. It recognizes no difference in the ability to sell books and the ability to sell ladies' underwear. An assistant buyer of books may be promoted to be buyer of lingerie and move from there to a post as merchandise manager for the Yonkers store. At least, within the Macy organization, salesmanship has been recognized as an empirical study, and the fact that Macy's training program graduates are in demand by department stores all over the country would lend credence to the belief that the entire department store industry has given tacit approval to this concept.

While the Macy training program is perhaps the leader in this field, other stores operate similar training programs that are only slightly less outstanding. Bloomingdale's and Abraham and Straus in New York, Marshall Field in Chicago, Wanamaker's in Philadelphia, and J. L. Hudson in Detroit offer training courses and recruit on the college campuses for personnel to fill them.

However, while the larger department stores offer opportunities for exciting and challenging jobs, this is not always true in the smaller, local stores. Often a local store is a family owned operation, and its scope of activities is not great enough to permit the promotion of outsiders to the better positions within the company. These stores may provide excellent service to the community and may provide a number of middle-management jobs to people of ability outside the owner's family. However, the student whose interests lie in the department store field should examine carefully the management structure of a small local store before he commits himself to a career within such an organization.

For many years, both Sears Roebuck and Montgomery Ward have conducted extensive college recruiting programs. These programs are similar in broad outline to the Macy program except that both of these operations have the added feature of an extensive mail order program. However, until recently, Montgomery Ward had an announced program of conservative development. This meant that the expansion of the Ward organization would be extremely slow and would be based upon only the most conservative estimates of the possibilities of the expanding economy. Sears, on the other hand, had an announced policy of maximum expansion that included not only new stores in the United States but a vast overseas program.

The college student who, in 1950, was offered similar training programs by both stores would have been wise to accept the Sears offer because it afforded a far better chance of advancement. If the company was going to expand, it meant that there would be a great many more opportunities with them than there would be with a "stand pat" organization.

Ward's has since reversed its position, but the example points out the importance of knowing something more about the organization for which you expect to work than the salary scale and extent of the fringe benefits.

It is unrealistic to assume that geographic considerations play no part in the young man's search for a place to begin a career. Home ties, financial considerations, and just plain old-fashioned sentiment quite often cause a college student to search for a place of employment near his home. Not all young men and young women can go to New York to take the Macy training course, and not all can go to Chicago to take the Marshall Field program. However, within the department store field, there is one chain that affords an opportunity for a graduating senior to pick up a training program near his home. The J. C. Penny operation, with 1,700 stores scattered across the country, often tries to place a trainee in a store in a locality close to the student's home. Assuming that a senior from Shaker Heights, Ohio, meets a J. C. Penny college recruiter at Brown University, it is quite possible that the recruiter will offer him a chance to take his training at a Penny store in the Cleveland area.

The training offered by Penny is not as comprehensive as that offered by Macy's or Marshall Field, but, then, Penny's is a slightly different type of store. Dealing mainly in ready-to-wear apparel, it has fewer merchandising problems and is more specialized in its approach to the sales problem. However, the individual entering any chain department store training program must realize that sooner or later he may have to move if he is to continue to advance within the organization.

This is a rule that is true not only of the department store industry but of all the big, nationwide industries. The people who man the middle- and top-management echelons of American industry have become nomads. They move from state to state at the dictates of the central corporation office. And they do it because it is to their financial benefit to do so.

Should a man refuse to move, it may mean that his promotions cease and that he will be frozen in his present spot from that time on. His only recourse in such a situation is to seek employment with another store or another industry within the same city.

However, matters such as these are of a personal nature and must be solved each time on the individual personality of the people involved. The young man in search of a career, however, should be made aware that this is a real problem and it is one that he will be forced to solve for himself should he choose to go to work for a national corporation.

Mail Order and Home Sales

In the modern age of super-markets, suburban stores, and easy transportation, it might reasonably be assumed that the mail order business would suffer a decline. But such is not the case. The big mail order houses of Sears Roebuck and Montgomery Ward are still going full blast with a sales volume that is greater than ever. The people who staff these operations are trained from the college-recruited training programs mentioned above.

Mail order sales, long in the book market, have recently invaded the phonograph record field, and other specialties such as the gift-of-the-month and the fruit-of-the-month are developing rapidly. The movement to suburbia has accelerated the mail order business. And the end is nowhere in sight.

The mail order business may well be the last stronghold of the rugged individualist. A glance at an advertising page of the home service magazines will show a fantastic array of mail order operations. At the same time, the book and record clubs afford classic examples of what mass advertising can do. Nothing tests the effectiveness of an advertising campaign as does the mail-in coupon at the bottom of the page. It is only a matter of time before the techniques now utilized so well by the book and record clubs are extended to such fields as silverware for young, unmarried girls, hobbies, and perhaps even ready-to-wear clothing.

Far from dead, the mail order business is only just beginning. And as it expands, it will utilize not the techniques of the retail store but the techniques of the advertising business.

Advertising

Perhaps no other business in America has had more unkind words written about it than has the advertising business. Some of this unkind comment has been deserved, and yet a great deal of it has been most unfair.

Some of the work of Madison Avenue has been in very questionable taste. Yet advertising has helped make the American marketplace the healthy place that it is today. It has been pointed out that the mail order business could not exist without the advertising man. There are other industries that are just as dependent on the toil of Madison Avenue—the cosmetic, the soap, the beer, the cigarette, the patent medicine, the woman's dress, the appliance industries— to name only a few. Without advertising to make the public dissatisfied with last year's style, with last year's vacuum cleaner, with last month's filter cigarette, many industries would wither and die.

It is admitted that there are abuses in advertising, but these are the abuses of an industry that has grown too fast for its own good. While there are abuses, there are also opportunities—opportunities for good jobs and opportunities for young men to grow up in an industry and to help it to find its proper share of social responsibility.

The advertising business is big—too big to be fully handled here. It is almost as complex as the automobile industry in the number of specialized jobs which it offers. It touches every person in America almost every minute of their waking hours.

For some occupations it represents the pinnacle of financial reward. For example, few artists outside of advertising manage to match the income of the top advertising artists. And it takes a really successful writer to earn more money than a crack, big agency copywriter. After these two occupations, advertising breaks down into two major fields (1) the salesmen who sell the services of the agency or who sell space in magazines and newspapers and time on radio and television and (2) the technical people—layout men, photographers, platemakers, media buyers, and a host of others.

As in all other fields, the salesmen draw the most money, and the salesmen who sell the services of the agency—the account executives—are at the top of the heap. At the bottom of the heap are the college recruited trainees who enter big agencies such as J. Walter Thompson, BBD&O, and N. W. Ayer and begin to learn the job from mail boy up.

The rules and regulations for advancement in an advertising agency cannot be written. Each young man will have to go where his talent takes him. Only in one relatively recent field can any background data be adequately sketched. The marketing and research sections of all advertising agencies are growing rapidly. In these positions knowledge in psychology, sociology, and research techniques are invaluable. In the fields of art and copy, the young man's talent will be the determining factor.

However, a word of caution is in order for any young man entering the advertising business. In this field, competence in a given specialty is highly rewarded, but the greater rewards go to the man who is able to see how all of the specialties fit together to form a completed advertising campaign. It is necessary for a young man to achieve excellence in a given specialty of the advertising business before he will be able to advance. But this advancement will be limited if he does not at the same time learn the other phases of the business. The account executive is usually the man who can fit all of the multitudinous pieces of the advertising business together in order to present a total picture to the client. It is a business that is never fully learned.

Advertising agencies range in size from large outfits such as J. Walter Thompson Company, employing several thousand people, down to local agencies which may have only three or four on the staff. Both have advantages and disadvantages. The danger of the big agency lies in the possibility of intense specialization—of the small agency, the lack of scope for real creative ability. But advertising is a game of individualists. It is not an easy field in which to get a start, and while a college degree is quite often required for admittance, this fact is quickly forgotten once the young man begins his apprenticeship.

The apprenticeship system still operates within advertising although it is seldom called by that title. It consists of working for low pay in a routine job within the big agency or of gaining similar experience at a local, small agency before moving to the big organization on Madison or Michigan Avenues.

There is another aspect of advertising that should be mentioned, and that is the opportunity that lies within the advertising department of every national and regional—and even some local—business operations. Such jobs afford the young man an opportunity to utilize his creative talents on a wide range of projects. Unfortunately, as a rule, these posts pay less than similar jobs with big advertising agencies. However, there are more of them.

Salesmanship as a Career

Within the American economy, as it is presently constituted, the salesman performs a vital function. He is his company's representative to the customer and on the success or failure of the salesman hangs the fate of all the workers in the factory. Without orders, the assembly line stops.

In 1958, the failure of the automobile industry to sell its predicted quota of cars was blamed in part for the recession of that period. The blame was placed—not on the workers and engineers who made and designed the cars—but on the merchandising men and sales departments who failed to sell them.

Such blame is a symbol of the importance of the salesman in the economy.

When the recession of 1958 did strike, every organization with a sales force held meetings to determine how its men could sell more effectively. Some organizations increased their sales and advertising effort. And this was happening while the assembly lines were slowing to a stop and unemployment figures were rising.

No greater proof of the importance of the salesman to the American economy is needed. It is unfortunate that the bad press that salesmanship has received over the years often discourages a young man from choosing sales as a career. Sales work is exciting, rewarding, and essential to our economic system.

CHAPTER SIX

FIGURES AND THE FUTURE

In any issue of *Fortune* magazine, there is almost certain to be an advertisement from one of the major manufacturers of office equipment depicting a giant automatic calculating machine. In the photograph at the top of the page, a well-dressed office manager will be pointing with pride at the gleaming pile of electro-mechanical machinery arrayed against the far side of the room. The office manager is talking to an older man who is obviously the president of the company.

"Our new super-computer saves us 210,000 man-hours a year," is the caption to the advertisement.

In any recent issue of *Business Week*, similar ads will show automatic machines saving thousands of man-hours per year in the engineering department, the payroll section, or the purchasing department of factories, insurance agencies, department stores, and research laboratories. In every case the emphasis in these ads is on the machines and away from people. If a human being does appear, it is made perfectly clear that this one person is actually replacing a half-dozen others.

But, while Madison Avenue has banished the individual from the paperwork operations of industry, the big corporations are still using them in great numbers. They may not be in the advertisements, but they are certainly in the offices. The man who saved 210,000 man-hours per year with his new super-computer neglected to say that the new machine was, for the most part, producing information that had never before been available to management.

The great value of the new automatic office machines is not that they reduce the number of people working for the company, but that they make it possible for management to have more information about every phase of their operation and to get that information faster.

Automation in the office now makes it possible to keep a daily inventory of all the materials in the plant, to compare stocks of raw materials in different divisions of the same corporation, and to correlate sales figures from across the country on a daily basis. All of this can be done with relatively simple punch card machines. By adding a computer to the mechanized office force, a corporation can use the data obtained from its office machines to develop equations that, when fed to the computer, will predict sales trends, estimate the size of a market for a given product, and develop pricing formulae. But the machines, as marvelous as they might be, will not make decisions. The human factor has not, and will not, be eliminated from the offices of industry.

The Accountant and Automation

What happens to the role of the accountant in this type of operation? The accountants of industry have usually come from the accounting and business schools, not the colleges of the country. And the controller of a corporation has come from the ranks of the accounting department. A surprising number of men holding controller's positions today are not college trained.

As the use of automatic office machines comes into more general use, the need for accountants will not be diminished in the least. It is possible that the increased scope of data produced by the machines will force the men in accounting departments to take a more comprehensive view of the company's operations. This will make it necessary for them to have a broader education than is now being given in the normal business school.

The new accountant will make a much larger use of statistics and economic theory. This will be brought about by the fact that more and more data will be handled by the accounting department. The traditional accounting procedures will remain, but they will be greatly augmented by statistical techniques made necessary by the use of large data processing office machines.

Accounting departments are not noted for their high pay scales. In fact, the sociologists usually refer to accountants when they want to point up the plight of the poor white collar worker. But automatic office machinery is already changing this concept. A company may have hundreds of thousands of dollars tied up in equipment rentals and it wants to obtain the maximum use of that machinery. To obtain maximum usage of these expensive machines, it must pay salaries that will attract top people. In organizations that have had a decade or more of experience with automated offices, this situation is developing. In companies only now converting to automated procedures, the traditional pay scales are likely to be changed.

Accounting departments also shy away from the establishment of training programs to aid young men to enter the better positions within the department. This, too, is certain to change as more and more automatic machines enter business and industry.

The introduction of electronics to the office has added the white coat worker to the white collar worker. These men are technicians trained by the manufacturer of the automatic equipment to see that the expensive electronic machines are always in top condition. In the larger organizations, these men are familiar not only with the physical machinery but also with the business procedures of the industry. In a few companies these are demanding, high-paying jobs.

Advancement in Accounting

In sections utilizing large computers, college trained mathematicians are used to "program" data for use by the electronic machine. Usually, the use of such computers is limited to the engineering and research sections. Only in the larger organizations do the statistical demands of the accounting department require personnel with college equivalent strength in mathematics.

The accountant, sitting at his desk with his comptometer, can look forward to very little advancement. Accounting sections are big and there are usually few supervisory posts. However, one escape valve does exist for the accountant in the form of the fiscal control sections that are common in many companies. This office, usually a staff function, is designed to act as a clearing house for management on all fiscal matters. It is concerned with such things as business trends, pricing structures, wage scales, and productivity rates. It often works closely with both production and personnel in addition to the accounting sections.

However, in the fiscal control sections, the accountant faces stiff competition because these groups recruit college men and train them for specialized staff positions.

The type of man who can best make his way in such a group is one who can combine both attention to detail and ability to see the broader scope of the company's total operation. These men are rare.

Before leaving the accounting department, it is necessary to mention the C.P.A., for a long time the top man in the hierarchy of accountants. The new automatic office machines are not likely to change his position. Books will still have to be audited by men. It is impossible to hold a machine responsible for a monetary shortage.

Cost Accounting

If the accounting departments do not offer good opportunities for the young college graduate, where is the business management major to find a niche in industry?

The modern factory has discovered the need for close cost accounting procedures and for an estimating section that can accurately fix the manufacturing costs of a product before it is sent to the shop for production. In some cases, the cost accounting section will be allied with the standard accounting department, but just as often it will be a separate section with a close working arrangement with the production groups. It is the function of the cost accounting section to obtain and to maintain records of the cost—in terms of labor and material—of each process in the manufacture of the company's products.

At the present time, some companies are actively recruiting college graduates for this type of work, although it is a position that has been traditionally filled by business school students or by clerks promoted from within the department. In those organizations with extensive training programs, a college graduate who enters such a program may find that the cost accounting section is one stop in his two-year tour of the various plant departments.

In a sense, the cost accounting section is the historical section of the plant, and the work requires a man who can give his full attention to details. It is an important operation within the framework of the total plant operation. Upon the detailed figures developed by this section depend the estimates on the production costs of proposed new products. Estimated production costs, in turn, affect the thinking of the sales department on price and possible market volume of the product. Cost accounting figures also play a big part in the company's attitude around the bargaining table at the time of new labor contract negotiations.

Within an accounting section, there is a decided danger that a young man can find himself trapped in the same position for a long period of time simply because he has mastered a given specialty. While it is, of course, important that any man perform his assignment to the best of his ability, it is equally important that he make every effort to learn as much as possible about the total operation of his section, his department, and his company. Over-specialization, without a compensating knowledge of the total picture, is almost certain to hinder the progress of any young man in business and industry. And this factor applies particularly to accounting.

Estimating

The estimating department is another section that presents a hazard in the form of over-specialization. However, the situation here is not as serious as in cost accounting. Estimating is an active assignment, bringing the young man into close contact with almost all phases of the plant operation. A good rule of thumb within all of industry is that the positions that permit a young man to establish contact with a number of sections—that permit him to be seen and observed by a variety of department supervisors—afford more opportunity for advancement than do assignments that keep him within the confines of his own department.

Industry does look for bright, young college graduates to work in estimating departments. But, for the first few years on the job, the young man will be given a variety of routine and even dull, detail work to do. This background of detail work is essential and there is no way that a good estimator can escape this apprenticeship.

The function of the estimating department is that of predicting, as closely as possible, how much it will cost the factory to produce a given product. In pursuance of this function, it must work closely with the production department, the purchasing department, planning and scheduling, personnel, and cost accounting. It is important, demanding work, and a good estimator is usually well paid. It is a job that, at times, forces a man to work under great pressure, and it is no place for a man with a thin skin. A sales manager can become very provoked with an estimating department that predicts a cost of production too high to make the company competitive in the field. And a plant manager can become equally excited when the estimate proves to be less than the actual cost of production on the assembly line.

Systems Control

The volume of paperwork in industry was large enough even before the introduction of the automatic data processing machines. Now there is more paperwork than ever. Systems control sections have existed in the larger factories for years. It is the function of these groups to design forms and procedures for the use of these forms in order that management can gather all the necessary information it needs about the operation of the factory. The demand of automatic business machines for vast quantities of data to digest and evaluate has only multiplied the importance of these sections.

Systems control sections of industry do recruit college graduates for their staffs. As a rule they are looking for business administration and business management graduates. Here, as in estimating, the young man will find that he must spend the first few years doing extremely routine work. The warning against over-specialization should be repeated here. A possible escape valve for the young man in this instance is to move to a post as administrative assistant to the supervisor of some large engineering or production section. Systems control is not an end in itself. It is simply a tool used by management to improve the efficiency of the plant. However, from the viewpoint of the college senior, it is a good place in which to observe the total plant operation.

Inventory Control

Inventory control is a function that is often attached to the purchasing department. The purchasing department is another section within industry that has traditionally not sought college-trained personnel. A buyer in purchasing usually began his career as a clerk in the office and worked his way through a series of promotions to his present position. From the company's standpoint, the greatest asset that a purchasing man can have is honesty. The temptations offered by salesmen are sometimes quite attractive, and they go far beyond a few drinks at lunch and tickets to the ball game.

The inventory control section within purchasing is primarily a record keeping operation that is staffed by clerical personnel. There are very few places within the plant that can utilize the talents developed by the purchasing buyer. Even the top men in such sections seldom move to higher posts within the company. However, buyers in many industries hold quite responsible positions and, unless a young man is positive that he has the makings of a vice-president, the position is often a satisfactory end in itself.

Traffic

Quite frequently, the traffic department is also attached to the purchasing department. This is another function that is normally filled by men who began in the plant as clerks. Occasionally, a worker will come off the loading platform to fill the job of traffic manager. It is an important post, and a good man on the job can make real dollar and cent savings for the company by the judicious selection of the proper carriers and the right shipping routes. It is also a place where a young man out of college might move rapidly because the competition is not overly keen.

Personnel

Somewhere along the way personnel work has obtained the reputation of being one of those jobs within industry that is both desirable and remunerative. Within reason, this is true. But it is also true that it is one field that attracts an inordinate number of applicants each year, and it is further true that there are many dull, routine, and unimaginative jobs within personnel work.

A young man often enters the personnel field because he is certain that he "likes people." He may take personnel administration in college or he may have studied business administration, business management, or business psychology. He may even have had a year or more of graduate school and be entitled to write M.A. after his name. The personnel sections are one phase of industry that actively search for people with graduate education.

Once inside the factory, the young man may find that he is assigned to interviewing applicants, or he may be sent out on the road to interview applicants in other cities or college students. Within a year or two, a young man may find himself back at his old campus conducting his own twenty-minute interviews with college seniors.

There are other jobs within the personnel section. The positions in the training sections have been covered in Chapter Ten. Other assignments might be found in wage and salary administration, in management development programs, and in the administering of employee benefit programs. As a rule, all of these jobs offer only average wages to beginners, and even the top jobs in these fields, except in corporation central offices, are likely to be moderate.

The best positions within a personnel section are in labor relations, but it is most unlikely that a young man just out of college will be assigned to this work. Recruits for labor relations work are usually drawn from the other groups within personnel. A man is moved into contact with labor union members only after he has proven himself to be thoroughly familiar with the policies of the company and has shown a genuine agreement with these policies.

Because of the need for labor relations personnel to be thoroughly familiar with the attitudes of union members, it is not unusual for management to move a highly successful production manager into this activity. The man may have no formal personnel training, but his record of handling workers, union representatives, and labor grievances qualifies him for the post. Training personnel, who have had experience working with worker groups, are sometimes moved over to labor relations before they reach the point in their careers of being considered for the top spot in the training department. Occasionally, a man from interviewing and recruiting may make the switch to labor relations, but men in wage and salary administration and employee benefits programs rarely make the jump.

Recreation directors and employee publication editors are two other personnel functions that rarely move into places of prominence at the union-management bargaining table. These jobs are further described in Chapter Seven.

But, since labor relations work requires a maturity that comes only with age and experience, the young man from college must resign himself to serving out his apprenticeship in one of the other groups within personnel work. He must always remember, however, that advancement is most promising in the area of labor relations, and he should prepare himself for a position in this group as soon as possible. Most Directors of Personnel come out of labor relations and, if the young man has his eye on the executive suite, the route leads through this group.

One factor must be remembered by every man in any personnel group. A personnel section exists for the purpose of improving the quality, increasing the rate of production, and reducing the cost of the product produced by the company. Boosting employee morale is good only when such a boost in morale will show dividends on the assembly line.

In the lower echelons of personnel work, it is quite difficult for a young man to keep from identifying himself with the people who come to him for help. If he has obtained a healthy dose of idealism while in school, this will be doubly difficult. But the good personnel man soon learns that he must acquire a sense of detachment from the other people in the factory.

A personnel worker must be sympathetic when an employee airs his problem but firm in administering the company's policies. It is one thing to "like people," but it is another thing when the young man feels the necessity for people to "like him." Such an attitude is a real handicap to good personnel people.

The young man who is assigned to wage and salary administration will find himself running surveys of wages in comparable industries and in different industries within the same geographic area. He will write endless numbers of job descriptions for the people in the plant. And few of the people for whom he prepares a job description will feel that he has been fair to their particular assignment. The information that he prepares will be passed on to the labor relations group and will be used at some later date in union-management negotiations.

The management development section within personnel is of comparatively recent origin. Usually this post is held by an older man who came to it through a staff position in management itself. In other cases a training director may be moved into the post.

The management development director is charged with the responsibility of finding likely prospects within the organization for supervisory posts. Once these men are located, the director recommends shifts in assignment, additional schooling, or other specialized training that will prepare these men for the day when they will take over the more responsible positions within the company. There is very little that the college senior can do to prepare for such a post.

Personnel work is interesting. It brings its people into contact with almost every phase of the company's operations. The personnel department is quite often the source of policy, and people working in personnel sections have a feeling of knowing what is going on throughout the company that is not shared by workers in other departments.

And there are excellent jobs within personnel. Most companies fully recognize the value of good labor relations, and they pay top salaries to top men to run their personnel sections. In recent years it has not been unusual for a vice-president in charge of personnel to be moved in as general manager or president of an organization.

There is one other factor that should be checked by the young man before selecting a specific position in personnel work. He should attempt to discover how much emphasis a given organization places on personnel administration. Many organizations may require personnel people but may not lay stress on personnel functions. Consequently, the salaries paid to personnel people are likely to be much less than in other organizations—automobile plants, steel mills, etc.—where good personnel work is highly regarded and highly rewarded.

Operations Research

Operations research is a new tool placed in management's workbox as a result of some very unorthodox study programs conducted by the British and American armed services during World War II. Basically, OR is an attempt to focus upon a single problem the talents of a great variety of professionals from a variety of fields. An operations research team could conceivably be made up of an historian, a physicist, a mathematician, a psychologist, and a cultural anthropologist. Its task might be to determine means of guiding ships through mine fields, of cutting down the length of the lines of automobiles at parkway tool booths, or of finding methods to determine, in advance, just how an individual soldier will behave under fire. All of these problems have been solved, at one time or another, by "opsearch."

At the present time, the biggest advocates of operation research are the armed services. For example, the Army commissions the Johns Hopkins University to solve some of its specialized military problems, and the Navy farms out similar work to M.I.T. But the number of operations research groups within industry is growing. Because it requires a large staff, or at least a variety of experts, to solve any one given problem using this method, operations research groups are limited to the largest companies.

Its interest for the college student lies in the fact that this type of work is virtually the only place within industry that makes use of many of the skills taught by the humanities. Certainly there are very few spots in business that have need for a cultural anthropologist. But OR has little room for the man with A.B. degree. The Ph.D is usually considered to be the minimal requirement.

And competition for the few existing jobs is keen. This is because OR people are in the forefront of experimentation with such exciting work as information theory, symbolic logic, and game theory.

Industry is developing more and more interest as operations research techniques are applied to such routine business administrative chores as supermarket operation, hospital operation, and the effect of promotional effort on sales.

The fact that positions in operations research usually pay more than strictly academic positions is also a factor in attracting good men to the field.

CHAPTER SEVEN

CAREERS FOR THE CREATIVE

GREAT INDUSTRIAL and business empires have long been patrons of the arts. But this patronage has usually taken the form of philanthropic investments in art museums, in colleges and universities, and in symphony orchestras. All of these very worthwhile philanthropies of big business are fine gifts to the community and to the nation, but their prime object is to preserve and to propagate the existing culture. Only a few industrial philanthropies, such as Ford, Carnegie, Rockefeller and Guggenheim, have expended much effort in developing fresh talent.

The young writer and the young artist have become accustomed to a view of industry very much like that of Charlie Chaplin's *Modern Times*. It is a place where men and women are chained to the steady forward movement of the assembly line. It is a place where the human factor is reduced to a mere cipher—a card in a time-clock rack. It is a place that stifles the individual, ruins initiative, and punishes individuality. In short, the young man who aspires to be a creative artist or creative writer stays as far away from the factory gates as it is possible for him to get.

However, in shunning the industrial scene, the creative individual may be passing up an opportunity to earn a lucrative living. This is not to say that industry has suddenly decided that it needs artists and novelists to become vice-presidents in charge of production. It is simply to state that there are good jobs for artists and writers in the advertising and technical publication sections of a large factory operation.

The Artist

Take the case of a young artist who is about to graduate from a good commercial art school or who was an art major in one of the many universities that now offer excellent art training. The choices that this young man has for employment are limited. If he is a serious artist, bent upon replacing Picasso and Utrillo in the museums, he knows that he has years of hard work ahead of him. In the meantime, he must earn a living.

The early years for the young artist are years of poor pay, even in the advertising business. While Madison and Michigan Avenues do pay well for top-notch advertising artists, they do not pay well for the beginner. And the top advertising agencies are located in a very few cities. Local advertising agencies in smaller metropolitan areas never do reach the point where they pay excellent wages to a creative artist.

The artist who has the determination to stick to his trade usually finds, after ten years or so at the drawing board, that his best move is to become a one-man art agency and to solicit work from a number of sources, do the work himself, and deliver it to the customer. He becomes a combination small businessman, artist, and errand boy. At this activity, the better free-lance artist can make a living—and a good one—but it is hard, time-consuming work.

The artist of exceptional ability, who is fortunate to find a berth with one of the top advertising agencies or lucky enough to break into the magazine illustrating field at an early age has gone a long way toward solving his financial problems. But, for others, the matter of earning an adequate living can be difficult.

Newspaper and department store art departments offer notoriously poor wages. The art labor market is further complicated by the fact that it attracts large numbers of talented young women whose wage demands are often less demanding than those of male artists.

All of which brings us to the positions that exist in industry for the artist. Industry requires large numbers of artists whose skills range from simple photo-retouching all the way to oil rendering. These people are employed in the advertising sections of an industrial organization, and even larger numbers are required in the technical publications sections.

These publications sections prepare all types of printed material, from safety posters for the plant bulletin board to instruction manuals on the operation and maintenance of the equipment produced in the plant. These manuals require every type of artwork imaginable—retouched photos, airbrush renderings, wash drawings, pen and ink sketches, scratchboard, water colors, and, in rare cases, oils.

And there are great quantities of this work. The young artist looking for a job where he will have an opportunity to develop his technical skill in any of the above art techniques will find that an industrial art section will give him all the practice he needs. The one thing that he will not get is an opportunity to give artistic treatment of the human form. His assignments will all revolve around mechanical objects—missiles, aircraft, tractors, radios, machine tools, etc.

For this work he will be well paid. A good artist, without supervisory responsibilities, can earn up to $7,500 in the larger industrial publications sections. A supervisor can earn as much as $10,000 a year.

For these wages, industry expects the artist to come to work at eight o'clock in the morning and to go home at four-thirty in the afternoon. He will also be confined to his art section and will be expected to produce a given amount of work in a week. However, industry does realize that the creative urge cannot be directed with the precision of an assembly line, and, except for occasional panics to meet a publication deadline, the industrial artist does not work under unreasonable pressure.

Not all industrial organizations maintain their own advertising or publications sections, and some have very small operations of this type.

As a rule, the better art positions exist in the larger industrial operations. Perhaps the best paying jobs of all exist in the airframe industry. The young man seeking an art job in industry must thoroughly investigate each company. Of great importance to the artist is the fact that the type of art work needed varies considerably from one company to another. But industry does offer real opportunities to the artist, and it is a field that should not be rejected without a thorough investigation.

The Writer

If the opportunities for the young artist in industry are good, then the opportunities for the young writer are almost unlimited. This state of affairs is brought about by the fact that the increasing complexity of industry is making unlimited demands upon the limited time of the executive. The many speeches, progress reports, magazine articles, and detailed policy statements that are expected of top management personnel cannot all be written by the same man if he is to satisfactorily perform his duties as an administrator. The factory manager who has time to write his own speeches for the local Chamber of Commerce meetings is a rare bird indeed, and the department chief who has the opportunity to pen his own annual report for the corporation's central offices is almost unknown. These men need the assistance of a trained writer.

In addition to the general ghosting of reports, articles, and speeches that goes on every day in any industry, there are a number of positions that call specifically for writers. Every plant with more than a thousand employees these days is likely to have an employee publication and to employ a writer to produce it. In the large industrial organizations, these publications are almost as expensive and as good as *Life* and *Scientific American.*

Just as the artist found opportunities in the technical publications sections of industry, the young writer can find similar work in these groups. The technical writer is a new post in industry, a job that grew up in World War II and, since that time, because of the bewildering complexity of the tools of war, has become an established part of the industrial scene.

The salary scale for technical writers is slightly below the scale for engineers, and, since engineering salaries are among the highest in industry, the technical writer fares very well. The technical writer does not require the same formal education as the engineer, but he does require some grounding in science. This means that he should have had the basic courses in these subjects. Perhaps the most important factor in the make-up of a good technical writer is a healthy technical curiosity. He must be capable of becoming interested in the "how and why" of the mechanical and electrical products produced by his employer. Without this curiosity, his work will be real drudgery and will never be first rate. With this curiosity, his work will be both exciting and rewarding.

Outside of the weekly paycheck, the technical publications sections of industry have much to offer the young writer. Perhaps the most important feature of a technical writing job is the fact that it forces the young writer to sit at a typewriter and to produce clear, readable prose. This sort of discipline is good for any young writer. If the young man is fortunate enough to find a technical writing section with a good editor who will point out his mistakes and guide him along the paths of good word craftsmanship, he is doubly blessed.

As with the artist, the problem of technical writing is that it deals with purely mechanical objects. Because it does not deal with the interplay of human emotions, it is not likely to develop the talents of the young man who is going to write the great American novel.

A second danger in technical writing is that the pay is good enough to tempt a writer to remain at this trade long after he has learned all that the job can teach him. The steady paycheck can look more important than the less certain, although more remunerative rewards, of free-lance magazine writing.

But the technical writer, unlike the technical artist, has an opportunity to move up into staff jobs within the organization. The most frequent move takes the technical writer into the post of staff assistant to the chief of an engineering department. And from there he can move to a staff assistant of a member of higher management. As was pointed out earlier, the men who run industry are always in need of a man who can shape their thoughts and ideas into some sort of readable prose.

The technical writer is also the man usually chosen to head up a technical publications section. Supervisory positions for artists are normally limited to direction of other artists.

A recent development in the technical writing field has been the increasing demand for men to write "proposals." These documents combine the talents of the technical writer and the advertising man to produce a report designed to convince a prospective customer—usually a government agency—that a particular firm is the right one to produce some new product.

The young man who decides to go into industry to edit a company publication will be in an excellent position to move on to better posts in administration. Only in rare cases, where the publication enjoys strong management support and a large budget, will the young man be satisfied to stay a house organ editor. Yet the nature of the work will take him into every section of the factory, and he will gain a fine working knowledge of just how things are done in almost every department. In many ways, editing a company publication is similar to a formal training program.

Unlike the student in the company training program, the editor has the added satisfaction of producing his weekly or monthly publication. He has an opportunity to write for an audience that will actually read what he has written. Company magazines are well read by the employees.

However, the editor also must face great frustrations in that almost every word that he writes will be subject to severe criticism by a long line of management members, from his section supervisor right up to the president of the organization. Editing a plant publication is no place for the young man with a crusading spirit. But it is a good place to get real practice at sitting at a typewriter. In many ways the plant publication is like a small town weekly. It has scoops, features, news stories, personals, and deadlines. And, if the young man can keep his sense of humor in the face of his multiple critics, it can be a lot of fun.

The man in industry who writes the speeches for the boss, who drafts the annual report to corporation headquarters on the factory's past accomplishments, who drafts the signed article for submission to a business publication is very seldom called a "writer" on the organization charts. Such a term would be very difficult to explain to the stockholders, and it would be almost impossible for the personnel department to write a job description for a ghost writer. But these men do exist, and they exist in fairly large numbers. Often they are tucked away in the Public Relations Department, but just as often they are a staff assistant to the factory manager, the vice-president, or the president.

But the ability to write well is usually rewarded in industry. The reason for this is that there are so few people who are capable of expressing their thoughts on paper. Since so much of the day-to-day activity of business must be carried on by means of the written word through reports, memoranda, articles, speeches, and letters, the man who can write has a decided edge on the man who cannot.

To the senior in college who is considering any post at all in industry, the best possible use for his senior elective courses would be to take as much English Writing as he can fit into his program.

Public Relations

Most industrial organizations of any size maintain a public relations office. Sometimes this office consists of one man, but, in the larger firms, it can be quite an organization. Its duties may range all the way from conducting tours of the plant for local civic groups to explaining to the local press why the workers in the factory have just gone out on strike. Somewhere in between, the public relations office tries to present a favorable picture of the company to the local community through newspaper stories, radio interviews, and even television shows. It tries to have the products produced by the factory announced and publicized in the business press. It may arrange shows and exhibits of the plant's products before trade and civic groups. In companies concerned primarily with products used by industry, the public relations office may also handle advertising. In factories producing consumer products requiring extensive advertising, the public relations-advertising functions are normally separate operations.

The young man entering such a section in industry can expect to be handed a wide variety of minor writing chores and an equally wide variety of leg-work setting up exhibits and shows. The salary paid industrial public relations men ranges from very good to almost poor, depending upon the stress laid by the company on public relations work. However, in this particular case, the college senior need not be overly concerned. Usually, it is only the more public relations-minded firms that send recruiters to the campus in search of talented college men. In the smaller organizations, the public relations man is more likely to be an older man who was appointed to the post from a staff position within the company.

Professional Positions

A big factory employing between 5,000 and 10,000 people will have almost as many different occupations represented on its payroll as exist in a small town. For example, there will be nurses, librarians, safety engineers, recreation directors, and teachers.

Most of these positions require special training and may be considered to be professional in nature. But industry makes demands upon its professional people that are not made outside of industry. These demands take the form of rigidly controlled working hours and adherence to the rules, so necessary in the operation of a factory but unknown outside the gates. In the case of teachers and recreation directors, a two-weeks vacation replaces the usual full season vacation normal in these professions. To compensate for the demands that it must make, industry makes one big concession—money.

In almost any factory, the plant librarian will make more money than her counterpart in the town library. The plant nurse is very likely to draw more money than a hospital R.N. The man who teaches foremen the rudiments of business management is apt to be far better paid than the teacher giving the same instruction in a small local college. The man who runs the plant recreation program will have a higher salary than the man with the same job in the city park service.

But the disadvantages of such jobs in industry are obvious. All of them are dead ends. There is only one librarian and the skills required by a good librarian have little application in any other section of the plant. The increased demand for technical personnel and the intense emphasis on all things technical has created a situation where even small industrial organizations require the services of a trained librarian. The demand has been so sudden and so complete that the library schools have not been able to supply enough graduates to fill the need. Traditionally, librarianship has been a woman's profession, with library schools graduating very few male students. The trend toward well-paying industrial library jobs may increase the number of male library school students. However, the great drawback for men will continue to be the fact that there is just no way to promote a librarian to a better job in industry.

The same factors are involved in the post of recreation director. A good athlete with a reputation gained as a college football hero can often find a well-paying berth in industry as the coach of the plant's sports teams. He will also be asked to supervise the company's bowling and softball leagues and any other recreation programs, from stamp clubs to model airplane building, that the employees decide they need. This, too, is often a dead-end job. Besides the fact that industry just has no way to promote a recreation director, the more conservative members of management often find it difficult to take seriously a young man who spends his time playing games. This attitude makes it hard for a recreation director to escape from his dead-end job into other phases of the company's operations.

The plant nurse is another field where the individual trades the prerogatives that usually go with her profession for the higher pay of the factory.

The underpaid school teacher who sees the industrial training director coming home every week with a fat paycheck may be quite envious of such a man. And it is a fact that industry does offer real opportunities in industrial teaching. As industry becomes more complex, the need for industrial training within the framework of the factory organization can only become more acute. Already some companies conduct training courses on a range of subjects from elementary soldering to advanced management techniques. Many plants are building classrooms as a matter of course and, often, these rooms are filled for the better part of every working day.

The classes are frequently taught on factory time, and the workers or supervisors are paid their regular salaries while attending class. Naturally, there is little truancy under such a system. Other courses are given at lunch hour or at the end of the working day with the company providing the teachers and the facilities. Attendance at these classes again is always high.

The industrial training director also acts as an advisor or counsellor to the employees of the plant. He must guide them in their selection of night-school courses that are available outside the plant and advise them on company policy pertaining to assistance to students.

The hours are more confining than those of the public school teacher, and the vacations are shorter. But there are no papers to mark at home—there is an office stenographer for such routine chores—and there are no P.T.A. meetings with irate parents.

Nor is the industrial teacher completely cut off from the type of academic research that is available to the public school teacher. There are professional organizations of training directors, and these organizations publish journals based on studies made by training directors in factories all over the country. It takes more than American industry to thwart the bent for educational research inherent in all teachers.

While no formal accreditation rules exist for teaching in industry, it is surprising how many training directors hold at least an M.A. in education. Apparently, teachers are teachers no matter where they work.

For the rugged individualist who is convinced that he is going to be a great artist, a great writer, or a teacher who will inspire future generations, industry can seem a confining, demanding master.

However, for the young man who needs a job while he is getting ready to set the artistic world on fire, industry can be a rewarding—and not an unpleasant—experience. Make no mistake, a job in industry is not a sinecure. The boss will expect a full day's work for a full day's pay, but that day's work is pretty much removed from the concept of the poor little man trapped by the moving assembly line in *Modern Times*.

In fact, life in industry is so pleasant that it can become a trap for the young writer or artist. The longer the young man stays in industry, the bigger his salary will become. And the more money he makes, the more difficult it will be for him to make the break and start out on his own as a free-lancer. Every industrial art department and every technical writing section has at least one man who is convinced that he could be a great artist or a great writer if only he did not need the money that comes in his weekly pay envelope. In the majority of cases, these men are kidding themselves.

The eight-hour day, five-day week is not so soul destroying that it prevents that same man from having an easel or a typewriter in his home. The man who is an artist or a writer does paint and does write. And he collects his weekly paycheck, too.

The truly creative man will find the way to be creative. A job in industry simply makes it possible to find his way without starving to death before he reaches his destination.

There are, of course, good jobs for creative people outside of industry. Everyone is familiar with the legend of the poor writer, starving in a garret while writing the great American novel. Then, one day, he sells his masterpiece to the Book-of-the-Month Club and to Samuel Goldwyn, and he retires to a villa on the Riviera. These opportunities still exist.

Magazines, Publishers, and Newspapers

There are also routine jobs in the publishing business. Every major magazine and every publishing house require a number of young people to serve as readers of manuscripts. These are normally low paying jobs from which the beginner is expected to reap his great rewards in "experience." In many cases, these jobs are reserved for women.

But there are other positions within the magazine field that attract writers and would-be writers. The news magazines use vast numbers of researchers, caption writers, and "junior" editors. Again, these are positions that are considered to be rich in "experience" rather than in salary.

It is in the field of trade magazines that the greatest number of writing jobs exist. These positions usually pay a trifle more than the routine beginner's assignment with the prestige, mass-market magazine, and they normally provide more opportunity for a young writer to actually see some of his material in print. The trade magazine field has seen tremendous expansion in the years since World War II, and, although the boom may be leveling off, this growth has greatly increased the number of opportunities.

Traditionally, young writers have gone into the newspaper business. In the past it was not unusual for a cub reporter to be paid $20 a week and be expected to work sixty or seventy hours. The newspaper guild has changed all that. Now the salaries for beginning reporters is far more reasonable, but the number of opportunities for young reporters is much less. Newspapers are using fewer cubs, and there are fewer newspapers every year.

The great value of newspaper work to any writer is the demand for great quantities of copy that publishing a daily newspaper requires. There is no substitute experience for being forced to sit at a typewriter to produce good, readable newspaper copy.

Needless to say, the competition for newspaper reporting assignments is quite stiff. And the college senior is unlikely to see a college recruiter from the *New York Times* or the *St. Louis Post Dispatch*. If a young man wants to become a newspaperman, he will have to make his own contacts.

CHAPTER EIGHT

A NATION ON THE MOVE

IF ANY ONE thing characterizes American life in the middle of the twentieth century, it is movement. More than ever before, Americans are shifting their homes about the nation in search of jobs during their working years and in search of leisurely living in their years of retirement.

This trend toward migration applies particularly to college graduates between the ages of thirty and forty. The young man who enters the large corporation with a middle-management or a top-management goal in mind must become reconciled to moving several times before reaching his ultimate goal. And these moves are not the normal shifts from one neighborhood to another as he climbs the corporation salary ladder. A young engineer, for example, may obtain his preliminary experience with a given company in a Long Island plant, be assigned to a minor supervisory post in a Florida operation, and finally move to a more responsible position in California or Michigan in the latter stages of his career.

Nor can the young man escape this modern nomadism by changing employers. The degree of specialization in today's industrial world seldom places more than one manufacturer of a given product in the same area. A man who becomes a sales executive in the appliance field may decide to give up his post with an upper New York State manufacturer only to discover that the comparable positions are with a company in Philadelphia or in the Mid-West.

In his fine book, *The Organization Man*, William H. Whyte, Jr.,[1]

---

[1] William H. Whyte, Jr., *The Organization Man* (New York: Doubleday Anchor Books, 1956), p. 298.

states that, within the twenty-five to thirty-four year age bracket, 45.5 per cent of all young people with at least one year of college training are at work outside of their home state. Of those who work their way through a college or a university outside of their home state, 69 per cent fail to return home.

At General Electric, the same book reports, a study of a cross section of thirty-five year old men showed that 58 per cent of these men had moved at least once during their career with the company.

This movement from one job to another, from one city to another, from one section of the country to another is changing many of the old social patterns of the country. But this is not a text in sociology. It is enough to point out that the young man's life with a major corporation is not likely to provide geographic stability.

Going hand in hand with the trend within corporations to move people about the country have been some rather large migrations of other segments of the population. Not all of the shifting population consists of college graduates seeking posts in the middle management of big business. Young men are still leaving the family farm to seek employment in the industrial cities. Negroes are moving out of the Deep South to seek jobs in the industrial centers of the North. Poor whites from the hill country of the Middle South are moving to large Midwestern cities, such as Detroit and Chicago. Puerto Ricans are entering the New York metropolitan area by the thousands. And the elderly retired citizens of the nation are seeking quiet homes in Florida and Southern California.

The Boom in Transportation

With such movements of population there is little wonder that the transportation system of the United States is experiencing a tremendous boom. And the population shifts are only one factor. When vacations and business trips between the various segments of scattered industrial empires are added, the volume in passenger traffic alone becomes staggering. Every mode of transportation, with the exception of certain rail lines, is experiencing an increase in passenger traffic. And this increase is continuing in spite of the diligent efforts of the automobile industry to convince every American family that it needs at least two automobiles in the carport.

In terms of freight traffic, the figures are even more impressive.

Even the railroads are carrying more tons of freight today than they did during the peak of the World War II activity. Airplanes are now seriously in the freight handling business, and the boom in trucking is apparent to anyone who has driven one of the big new inter-state parkways in the last few years.

Recruitment and Training

With transportation experiencing such a tremendous growth, it would seem logical that this would be an excellent field for the college graduate. This would appear to be a business that, because of its great expansion, should provide great opportunities for a young man to grow as the industry grows.

All of this is true. But it is true only in a limited sense. Traditionally, the transportation industry has not recruited college graduates. And, while this attitude is slowly changing, the transportation industry does not offer the neat little slots into which college graduates fit so nicely in other segments of the economy.

It is true that a number of colleges and universities are offering courses in transportation, traffic management, and allied subjects. Some are even offering full four-year programs in this area. The state universities have given particular emphasis to transportation as a career. Yet the transportation industry itself has paid very little attention to this form of college training. One major eastern railroad has a definite policy of not hiring graduates of these transportation courses. Other railroads do hire college men with a degree in transportation, but the opportunities offered to them are often no better than those offered an alert, keen, high-school graduate who is willing to apply himself diligently to the job.

A student in a college or a university not offering any specific courses in transportation is unlikely to see very many recruiters from the transportation industry. And even students in schools with such study programs are not going to be overwhelmed with offers.

The Airlines

Of course, the most dramatic phase of American transportation has been the spectacular growth of air travel. At the pilot level, the airlines offer some of the most attractive jobs anywhere in American industry. Because of feverish activity by the pilot's union, these men can earn $20,000 a year, or more, for a greatly abbreviated work week. As the use of jets becomes more common, the salary scale for pilots can only increase.

However, as the salary scale for flying personnel has increased, so have the requirements. At this time, almost the only way in which a young man can amass the number of flying hours required to qualify for an airline pilot's job is through some time in the armed services. Since the services require at least two years of college for their flying school candidates, a young man seeking a commercial pilot's job can consider his hitch in the Air Force as graduate training. But there can be many a slip in the service. A young man entering the Air Force or the Navy can have no positive assurance that he will be assigned to the type of work that will enable him to apply later for the commercial job. But the final goal is attractive enough to make many young men take the risk. Actually, the risk is small. The young man who is completely wrapped up in aviation will not be unhappy in the Air Force, even should his plans for a career in commercial flight fail to materialize.

There has been a rather strange phenomenon develop as a result of the very high salaries paid to commercial pilots. Ever since the days when airplanes were flown by the "seat of the pants," the pilot has been the top man in the social hierarchy of flight. He naturally gravitated to the better administrative posts with the airlines. This is no longer an attractive move for the experienced pilot. His salary as a pilot, combined with his short working hours, quite often makes a desk job at a comparable wage seem like a demotion. This has opened the way for nonflying personnel to move into administrative posts on the ground.

The airlines, almost alone of all the transportation fields, have seriously recruited students on the campus. The glamour of the age of flight has attracted many young men. But the assignments open to these college-trained young men have not always proven to be full of excitement. Air travel, like all forms of transportation, is a service industry, and the beginning positions in the field are mostly of a routine nature. Checking flight lists, establishing baggage handling procedures, and placating irate customers who cannot get a seat on the 1:15 to Chicago will, after a few years, begin to dampen the ardor of the most enthusiastic supporter of air transportation.

In their recruiting operation, the airlines look for A.B. graduates to enter an eighteen months training program. The first eight months of this training is spent orienting the new employee to all phases of the airline's operation. This is followed up with a month or two of formal instruction at the central headquarters of the company, and the final six months is actually spent behind the counter at a ticket office. There is no way to escape this stint as a ticket salesman because the airlines feel that this is not only good training for the new employee but is a vital part of the air transportation industry.

The first permanent assignment for the young man after the completion of his training program will, again, be in the area of ticket sales. This time he will be placed as a first line supervisor at one of the airline's ticket selling operations. Here he will spend three or more years before moving on to other assignments in sales work or in the operations end of the business.

While some of the supervisory assignments at the major air terminals of New York, Miami, Chicago, and Los Angeles carry heavy responsibilities and satisfactory salaries, there are far more assignments in minor metropolitan centers where there is little traffic and many routine chores.

As the volume of air traffic grows, some of the major airlines are discovering the value of industrial engineers to study such things as scheduling, freight handling procedures, and plans for further expansion. In the maintenance shops, industrial engineers are employed to reduce the turn-around time of an aircraft. But these young men are on the scene only in small numbers, and there is no defined path that a young man can follow in order to arrive at such a post.

Yet the importance of air travel continues to increase. As the major airlines become more and more concerned with jet travel over the more productive routes, feeder airlines will grow to take up the burden of short trips between cities less than 500 miles apart. The helicopter is only just out of the barnstorming stage, but, within a few years, it should be a regular feature on the air transportation scene.

It is this growth of feeder airlines and helicopter service for short trips that will further cut into the passenger traffic of the railroads.

Already some serious observers on the American scene are predicting that the railroads will go out of the passenger business completely within the next twenty years.

The Railroads

The American railroads have so many problems that it is difficult to know where to start in describing them. Not the least of their difficulties is the great quantity of antiquated rolling stock now owned by the roads. The box car, the stable carrier of the railroad, has changed very little in the last century. And the roads have literally hundreds of thousands of them. Any attempt to introduce new shipping techniques to the railroads is always slowed by the necessity of maintaining the existing equipment while, at the same time, introducing the new. This often means two sets of operating procedures with its resulting increased cost of operation. It is, of course, economically impossible to replace all of the existing rail equipment at one time.

Not only is the equipment of the railroads antiquated, the personnel of many systems are equally out of date. Railroading is the oldest segment of the American transportation complex, and it has had many years in which to develop traditions that are difficult to break, even though these same traditions no longer serve the railroads in the modern era. Railroad unions are also quite strong, even in the white collar field, and these unions are careful to protect their membership against developments that might tend to eliminate any positions.

Because the railroads have been operating for a long time, the men in the top supervisory positions are likely to be older than men of equivalent rank in the newer transportation fields, such as aviation. These men have a tendency to look twice at any new plan that might disrupt the traditional pattern of operation.

The railroads themselves are quite aware of their shortcomings and their personnel problems. They are very much aware that improvements must be made if they are going to continue to compete with the newer transportation fields. To help solve their problems, most of the larger roads now have established departments to solve the technological and procedural problems of rail transportation. Industrial engineers are in service, and data processing equipment has been installed in an attempt to handle the tremendous amounts of paperwork generated by rail shipments. Television has been installed in marshalling yards, a piggy-back system has been developed to ship trailer trucks by rail via flat cars, and sea trains are being used to transport large numbers of box cars from one railroad to another.

The demand for engineers in all segments of industry has forced the railroads to recruit college seniors for these posts. Railroads have need of civil engineers to work on their roadbeds, their bridges, and their tunnels. Their recent excursion into the field of automation and electronics has brought about the need for electrical engineers. Much of the engineering work with the railroads is of a practical nature, and very little development work, and almost no research assignments, are available. Some roads have training programs lasting up to two years to offer young engineers.

However, even within the engineering field, the recruiting of college-trained engineers by railroads is limited. Many roads are making no moves at all in this direction, even though many of them realize that they are going to be forced to such a program within the next few years.

But, other than in the engineering fields, the railroads have done little or no recruiting. In the past they have stressed security on the job, but the publicity resulting from the cancellation of a number of passenger lines and the state of the railroads in general has weakened this picture in the mind of the public at large. Within the clerical departments of the railroad, it is still common for a young man to start as a mail boy and work his way up through the ranks. This possibility hardly inspires a college senior with real fervor.

However, the railroads are working hard to establish new sections to revamp their old procedures and, for such sections, are looking for industrial engineers and cost accountants. Graduates in business management and business administration are likely to find less opportunity with railroads than with industrial and business operations of similar scope and size.

Trucking

One of the major factors worrying the railroads as they look toward the future is the spectacular growth of the trucking industry. The truckers have made tremendous strides in the years since the end of World War II, but, again, trucking is a field that has traditionally drawn its employees from outside the ranks of the college graduate. There are almost no training programs, and the pay, for all skills except that of driving a tractor trailer, is likely to be below that of industrial corporations.

A few of the more public relations minded trucking firms have established scholarships at the college level, but the place of the college trained man in the trucking industry remains clouded. The trucking business is one of the few remaining spots within industry and business that has space remaining for the small entrepreneur. A man with a few thousand dollars can actually get into the trucking business on a small scale, and, in fact, many of the companies now owning fleets of trucks began in just this way.

Because there are a large number of independent trucking firms traveling over the same highways, the competition is very strong for the existing business. Consequently, some of the larger firms offer some excellent opportunities in sales. In the smaller firms, sales jobs are not likely to pay too well, and the opportunity for the young man in these cases is contingent upon the success of the total trucking operation. If the line prospers, the salesman is very likely to be well rewarded. If the line fails, there is going to be very little opportunity for anyone connected with the operation.

A corollary of the mass migrations mentioned earlier in the chapter has been a boom in the moving business. This, also, is highly competitive and requires good sales personnel. However, this is another field that has not, in the past, drawn its personnel from the college ranks.

Buses

Buses are one of the big reasons why the railroad passenger business is in serious trouble. More and more inter-city bus lines have, through lower fares and more frequent schedules, cut heavily into the rail passenger traffic. In operation, the problems of the bus lines are similar to those of the airlines. In terms of scheduling, baggage handling, and specialized freight handling, the problems are almost identical. Bus fares are correspondingly less than those charged for air transportation. While the passenger traffic volume is much greater on the bus lines, there is still little margin in the operation for high salaries. As in the other fields of transportation, bus lines have not recruited on the college campus.

The College Graduate in Transportation

Perhaps one of the reasons for the lack of interest in college graduates on the part of the transportation industry has been the rapid growth of the industry. This growth has been so rapid that the various airlines, bus lines, and truckers have not had the opportunity to thoroughly study their over-all operations and determine just where more highly skilled personnel could be used to better advantage. The older railroads have made these studies, but their problems are far deeper than simply finding spots for more highly trained employees.

From the above, it would appear that there is little room in the transportation field for the college-trained man. This is not true. There is simply no formal program designed to fit the college graduate similar to those that exist in almost every other field. Because there is no formal pattern for the young man with advanced training, it does not mean that there is no place for him in the industry.

Certainly no spokesman for the transportation industry is going to state that his industry is not searching for good, alert, well-trained people. Every industry is on the lookout for this type of person. The transport industry has not reached the stage of development where its organization has become rigid and formalized. A young man with drive, determination, and the ability to act on his own initiative is quite likely to advance in this field for the very reason that he will stand out from the other employees around him.

If college is to teach a man how to think and how to act on his own, then a college education will be far from wasted in transportation.

CHAPTER NINE

WHERE THE FUTURE IS BRIGHTEST

ONE OF THE underlying themes of this book is that the American economy will continue to grow. This is not an unfounded optimism. The population explosion described in Chapter Ten will not only increase the demand for teachers; it will also increase the demand for lawyers, doctors, engineers, accountants, bankers, writers, salesmen, production experts, and all of the other trained people who make up our modern society.

But population growth is not the only factor affecting career opportunities in the years ahead. The great technological advances that are being made every day are reshaping the future even as this is being written. Fifty per cent of the products currently being manufactured by General Electric were not even in existence twenty years ago. Change is destined to be our companion in the years ahead, and in America change has always meant growth.

The remainder of this chapter is composed of statements by leaders of some of the most important corporations in America outlining the career possibilities for young men in their industries during the next decade. To a man, these business leaders foresee a steadily increasing demand for college trained young men. These statements were prepared specifically for *The Twenty-Minute Lifetime*.

AIRCRAFT AND MISSILES

FRANK PACE, JR.
President
General Dynamics Corporation

I know of no industry during the next decade that will offer the tremendously challenging and expanding opportunities to be found in the aviation and missile industry. It encompasses the widest range of the sciences and engineering disciplines such as aeronautical, chemical, electrical, mechanical and nuclear engineering, physics, chemistry, and mathematics. Here is an industry that is reaching into the new frontiers of space for new means of propulsion. Needs for the technical men are particularly great but great also are the opportunities for the non-technical graduate in administrative and other basic non-technical phases of the business. There are, moreover, magnificent opportunities for graduates to gain new knowledge and techniques in areas as yet uncharted and barely dreamed of.

The pursuit of these horizons, of the mind as of the physical universe, will result in accomplishments which will profoundly affect the way of life of people everywhere. Participation in an area of endeavor which is so intimately associated with man's yearning for peace, knowledge, and progress affords an outstanding opportunity for a life of continued individual growth and sense of excitement. This, plus a sense of contribution to man's progress, is what makes for a career of satisfying accomplishment.

ATOMICS

WALTER S. BAIRD
Chairman
Baird-Atomic, Inc.

The words "atomic" and "nuclear" have become a part of our daily life, but few people not directly concerned, even in the fields of science, seem to have any realization of the revolution going on around them, as expressed by these two words.

In the atomic research field alone the number of possibilities have grown exponentially during the last ten years and with practically no limit in sight. The explosion of the hydrogen bomb has opened up complete new areas for investigation, these to do the same for the fusion process as has been done for the fission process. Research in this particular area is today, and probably will be for a number of years ahead, much more exciting largely because there are so many unknowns between science as it now stands and the predictable control of a process already proven by the hydrogen bomb.

If we will look at the by-products of the reactors and piles, we have now a whole new field of technology best illustrated by the use of isotopes to measure the rates of reaction of physical, chemical, and biological processes. The very understanding of these reactions and the measurement of them is expanding our frontiers in power development, medicine, and agriculture in a way so rapidly unfolding that it is almost impossible for even the universities to keep abreast.

At the same time this work is going on, the engineering phases are following with just as high a degree of intensity. This naturally leads to a whole new technology having to do with making these products useful; for example, the making of cheap power, the better use of our soils, the better growing of foodstuffs, and the treatment of diseases.

Career opportunities in this new age will be limited only by the willingness of students to recognize and prepare for it, no matter into what phase their future interest may take them, whether it be research in any of the fields mentioned above or in the supporting technologies.

THE AUTOMOBILE INDUSTRY

FREDERIC G. DONNER
Chairman
General Motors Corporation

In America, as in no other country, the automobile is an integral part of our social and economic life. With our healthy population growth and rising incomes, with an accelerating trend toward suburban living and multiple car ownership, with the development of a greatly improved network of highways, the automobile industry can look forward to substantial growth over the next decade.

This growth will be reflected in rising employment and particularly in more white collar as opposed to blue collar jobs. Because of the increasing complexity of our products and of the machines that make them—and also because of the increasing complexity of business itself—the percentage of highly trained people to the total number of men and women on our payrolls has been steadily increasing. This trend can be expected to continue.

Our greatest need over the next decade will be for college graduates with degrees in engineering and science—and more specifically for those with degrees in electrical and mechanical engineering, in physics, and in mathematics. We shall need the physicist for our research projects, the math major for our analogue and digital computers, and the electronics engineer for the many devices installed in our products and for operating our machines.

Another area of growing opportunity is accounting and finance. Business Administration graduates with masters' degrees in accounting and corporate finance will be increasingly in demand in the business management area.

The automobile industry will continue, of course, to have many job openings for other engineering specialists as well as for chemists, industrial designers, and just plain liberal arts graduates. But the greatest opportunities in the decade ahead will be found in the fields I have emphasized—electrical and mechanical engineering, physics and mathematics, and accounting and finance.

BUSINESS MACHINES

RAY R. EPPERT
President
Burroughs Corporation

The next ten years will see the need and use of automatic and semi-automatic data processing equipment multiply many times in our nation's offices, factories, stores, and banks. In supplying this need, America's office equipment industry cannot help but grow.

The reasoning is simple. The increase of population alone, with its accompanying expansion of economic activity, will multiply the need for quick, accurate, economical data processing systems for handling the rising flood of paperwork. Added to this is the growing demand for precise and reliable computing and recording equipment, so vital to our national defense and the coming space age.

At the present time, more than 250,000 persons in the United States of America are engaged in the fields of data processing equipment for business as well as electronic devices for defense.

Although competition in the labor market will be strong, in the years ahead, there will be little call for the second-best or the poorly prepared. Standards are high and must go higher for engineers, research workers, marketing, sales and service experts, specialists in manufacturing methods and product planning. As new areas for development are opened, new specialists will need to be trained.

Above all, the office equipment industry, like other key American enterprises, will need a reservoir of capable, well-educated leadership to maintain the sound, dynamic growth we must have to keep pace with a growing America.

THE CHEMICAL AND DRUG INDUSTRY

THOMAS S. NICHOLS
Chairman
Olin-Mathieson Chemical Corporation

One cannot speak of chemicals and drugs as one can, for example, of automobiles and steel, as constituting a single industry. The manufacturer of cosmetics is not in the same industry as the supplier of high energy rocket fuels to the government. He will offer different opportunities and will appeal to different types of young men and women. Nevertheless, it is, I think, fair to say that the chemical and drug field, broadly defined, offers as many opportunities and challenging careers as any. After all, such unrelated but exciting problems as those involved in curing cancer and conquering the moon will be solved largely through chemistry.

Advances in the field of chemistry will continue to make possible new industries and to open up new careers. Almost all types of specialists will be required from agronomists to zoologists but the most interesting and rewarding jobs will not be available to a man just because he is a research chemist or an engineer or an accountant. These jobs will be reserved for the men and women who, whatever their field of specialized training, can evaluate the effects on our economy of the constantly accelerating advances of chemical knowledge and related technology. Chemical discoveries have always influenced man's economic development, even his culture and social habits. They will continue to have an increasing impact on our civilization and, in a very real sense, to change our lives. The future of every chemical company must depend on those who have the ability to recognize and seize opportunities from this impact and these changes.

A great deal has, of course, been written about the glamorous aspects of the chemical business. Most of it is quite true. Yet, I believe, one of the best ways for a young man to start his career in the chemical field is by getting to know the relatively prosaic heavy chemicals. In 1843, the German chemist, Liebig, wrote: "We may fairly judge of the commercial prosperity of a country from the amount of sulphuric acid it consumes." Today, as much as ever, alkalis and heavy chemicals are the workhorses of the industry. They are sold on a repeat business basis composed of a relatively few number of customers who, however, are industrial "blue chips."

The man who sells sulphuric acid or caustic soda, for example, has to learn the business of each of his customers and the relationship of the customer to its industry. After a while, if he is bright and hard-working, the young man in this line of work can learn a great deal. He can acquire a considerable knowledge of our basic industries, a unique understanding of the problems and potentials of its diverse units and considerable insight into the fascinating inter-relations between various products and markets which, on the surface, are entirely unconnected. This background will be of immense value to him during his entire business career.

THE CONSTRUCTION INDUSTRY

A. R. FISHER
Chairman and President
Johns-Manville Corporation

As America's biggest industry, construction is one of the major props of our economy. It accounts for about 15 per cent of the total output of goods and services in the United States.

Private construction, for example, includes new homes, hotels, plants, stores, restaurants, garages, offices, churches, schools, hospitals, farm buildings, utilities, and institutional, social, and recreational structures.

Public construction embraces plants, military and educational facilities, hospitals, highways, sewer and water systems, and conservation and development projects.

In 1959, out of an estimated gross national product of about $480 billion, new construction will account for about $50 billion, and maintenance and repair of existing structures about $20 billion. By 1970, it is estimated that the annual volume of construction will be about twice that amount.

As a result of the high birth rate in the 1940's, family formations will boost demand for homes in the 1960's. Technological advances and a continued rise in the American standard of living are also factors that will spur construction.

Thus the construction industry offers many opportunities. It is so broad in scope that it will require the talents of highly trained men and women in such diverse fields as sales, manufacturing, research, engineering, architecture, business administration, finance, and community and highway planning.

For its part, the building industry is constantly striving for better home styling, uniform building codes and zone rules, more attractive home financing, and new and improved building materials, all with the objective of giving the homeowner more value for his dollar.

THE ELECTRONICS INDUSTRY

JOHN L. BURNS
President
Radio Corporation of America

The electronics industry has grown in the past twenty-five years from virtually nothing to fifth place among American industries. Its total annual volume—including manufacturing, broadcasting, distribution, and servicing revenue—is more than $12 billion, and indications are that it will at least double that volume in the next ten years. Thus electronics is one of this nation's major growth industries and will offer increasing opportunities for young men in engineering, research, manufacturing, sales, merchandising, and business management.

Electronics is vital in modern methods of communication and mass entertainment. National defense depends on it to an increasing degree, and the armed forces are the industry's biggest single customer.

Electronic devices and systems are finding their way into many new phases of industry as the automation of manufacturing and office procedures increases. The next decade will see vastly increased application of electronics to the fields of medicine and educational television. The exploration of space has opened a new and fascinating phase of electronics engineering.

The best available estimates of manpower in the electronics industry indicate that it employs about 1,500,000 workers today. This includes some 50,000 scientists and engineers—roughly 3 per cent of the total.

This year the industry expects to get from the universities about 4,000 scientists and engineers qualified in electronics. It is probable that 15,000 could be used if they were available with the right specialties.

All indications point to a vastly expanded job market over the next five to ten years, especially for scientists and engineers with advanced degrees. In no phase of American industry are the opportunities more varied, more interesting, or more vital to the prosperity and security of the nation.

THE FOOD INDUSTRY

PAUL S. WILLIS
President
Grocery Manufacturers of America, Inc.

The food industry has enjoyed a phenomenal growth particularly since 1939. Fifty years ago—in 1908—consumer expenditures for food totaled $7 billion. In 1939, this volume totaled $16 billion. From there on, the business has really moved forward, reaching about $75 billion in 1958. We expect that by 1965, food volume will reach $100 billion.

The food industry has become a big industry in every sense of the word. It is not only the nation's largest industry in terms of sales, but it has dignity and the respect of the American people. It provides opportunities for creativeness on the part of its people, and it offers both high and steady incomes.

To understand the future job opportunities in the food industry, it is helpful to understand why this business has grown. The increase in population and national income have, of course, contributed, but the industry's expansion has been far greater than can be explained by those factors alone. There are many reasons for this plus growth, but chief among them have been:

1. The tremendous flow of new and improved products created by the research and development of grocery manufacturers;
2. The efficiency of wholesale and retail distribution operations with their beautiful supermarkets where a large assortment of offerings attractively displayed tempt consumers to select the brands and products they like to buy;
3. The development by both manufacturers and distributors of sales, advertising, promotion, and merchandising techniques which fit in with the modern methods of self-service distribution and the dynamic potentials of a growing America.

What does all this mean in terms of job opportunities in food manufacturing companies? Because of the rapid introduction of scientific processing equipment, it may not mean more total jobs in production. With the growth of large retail stores, it may not even mean more total jobs in sales. But it certainly does mean there will be more *good* jobs—more jobs demanding higher training. That will probably be true in the scientific research and development area which is concerned with the physical, chemical, and nutritional aspects of creating the new and improved products on which the industry's future depends. It will probably be even more true in all the areas which are part of marketing—sales, advertising, promotion, consumer and marketing research, packaging, transportation, etc. Food manufacturing has become a scientific operation in all of its aspects, and we foresee a growing opportunity in all branches of company operations for the intelligent, ambitious, industrious and well-trained man or woman.

THE INSURANCE BUSINESS

CARROL M. SHANKS
President
*The Prudential Life Insurance
Company of America*

The insurance industry in all of its branches is a story of dynamic growth. As our population and gross national product go up, there is an ever-increasing market for insurance protection. This means that there will be rapid expansion in both the field and home office forces of the industry. This expansion is visualized not only for the next decade but for many years to come. Growth means opportunity for the young men and women of America to build themselves satisfying and rewarding careers in a field that is vital to the economy of our country.

Many people think primarily of the salesman when insurance careers are discussed. He certainly is a most important figure in the industry. But there is a tendency at times not to remember the administrative, professional, and technical members of the team who back up the agent in bringing service to the public. The general field of insurance is so broad that careers in many different types of activity are available to outstanding young people. To mention only a few, insurance companies need actuaries, accountants, auditors, investment analysts, methods consultants, underwriters, and specialists such as doctors and lawyers. Development and training in these various fields can lead to positions of high-level management or technical responsibility.

The insurance industry takes care of its own. The top executives of tomorrow in this field will come from the group of promising young people who each year are starting their business careers in insurance. In the growth situation that constantly faces us, there will be more and more room at the top for the individual who demonstrates real ability.

MACHINE TOOLS

MOREHEAD PATTERSON
Chairman
American Machine and Foundry Company

The machinery industry is a growth industry. The rapid and continuing increase in the standard of living, both in the United States and throughout the world, has been brought about and will continue to be primarily caused by the introduction of new machines. Coupled with the explosive increase in world population, the rising standard of living demands more and better goods and services for more people. Increased mechanization, the machinery industry's answer to this demand, provides finer quality and higher quantity output with fewer man-hours of labor.

In this blasé age, when "automation," "electronics," "satellites," and "space vehicles" have become household words, it is worth reflecting on the fact that our progress is primarily traceable to advances in the machinery industry, brought about by dynamic young people who were too foolish to recognize that "it couldn't be done," and supported by imaginative management which was willing to take a chance on new ideas.

Historians looking back at the 20th Century may well conclude that economic expansion was one of its major characteristics. There is every reason to believe that the accomplishments of the second half of this century will be even more important than those which we have already seen. The challenge of the tremendous pressures for reduction of working hours and for more industrial output for more people will be met by the machinery industry. Drastic changes in production methods are occurring with increased frequency; fantastic though it may sound, industry will literally be using robots to replace men for simple repetitive tasks within the next ten years. Machine tools are already turning out finished items with only nominal supervision, and other machinery is replacing humans for such unlikely tasks as setting up bowling pins.

The growth of the machinery industry is keyed to the inevitably rising standard of living for a growing world. World population is presently increasing at a rate which adds to the globe the equivalent of a new nation the size of the United States every four years. If there were no change in the standard of living, this new world population would require 2 per cent more goods and services per year, but, coupled with the increased demands of all the people for better living standards, the machinery industry faces a major growth situation.

The machinery industry needs people with intelligence, imagination, and drive if we are to keep up this ever-increasing pace of better quality and higher quantity production at lower unit cost. The demand for higher and higher standards of living by more and more people will not allow our industry to rest on its laurels. To survive, a company must keep moving with this tide. We need scientists and engineers of all types to develop new products and improve our present lines; we need manufacturing men who can turn out our products on a competitive basis; we need men who can plan, who can sell, and who have the vision to see new needs and wants so we can provide new products. From these men we expect to find our future business leaders—the men who must have the imagination and the daring to continue and improve upon the progress which our present management and the management before us has made.

THE PETROLEUM INDUSTRY

W. ALTON JONES
Chairman
Cities Service Company, Inc.

Few industries in America rival petroleum in the wealth of opportunities it offers those who serve it well. Exploration, production, transportation, manufacturing, marketing, research, administration —these activities invite the talents of chemical, mechanical, civil, electrical and petroleum engineers, chemists, physicists, geophysicists, geologists, salesmen, economists, and men trained in law, accounting, and industrial and public relations.

In recent years, the civilized world has moved toward an oil economy. Even the advent of nuclear energy seems unlikely to slow this pace in the foreseeable future.

The history of petroleum has been one of dynamic growth. Petroleum has paced the progress of industry, transportation, and agriculture. It has added a multitude of conveniences to modern living. It is one of man's most useful servants.

Petroleum research, for example, is a major industry in itself. It has developed almost countless new products and uses for oil. Each new development, each new discovery, opens a new field of opportunity and a new challenge to American youth. Consider, as an instance, the dramatic progress of petrochemicals and the impact of products made from petroleum upon the American standard of living.

Present plans of the industry reflect the full faith of its leaders in petroleum's future. To realize these plans, there will be growing need for men and women trained and ready for exacting assignments. In the tradition of the industry, these people will share the gains they help make possible—and if the goals of the industry are fully realized, these gains will be great indeed.

RETAILING

J. GORDON DAKINS
Executive Vice-President
National Retail Merchants Association

Retailing is a big industry. There are more than 1,700,000 retail establishments in the United States—42 per cent of all the individual business organizations in the country. They require the services of 8 million individuals. Collectively, this vast organization constitutes one of the most important economic activities in this country. Notice, too, that the retail business has grown substantially through the years. Back in 1939, total retail sales amounted to $42 billion. Last year they reached $200 billion.

Retail stores now supply 90 per cent of all the things we need for the homes we live in, the food we eat, and the clothes we wear. Retailing is a big industry in every sense and is constantly expanding. Since 1929 the number of people in retailing has just about doubled. New stores of all kinds are opening every day, creating more and more opportunities for career-minded young people.

The future looks bright for people coming into retailing now. Our population is growing at an unprecedented rate. Newer and bigger stores will be needed to keep pace. The very fact that retail sales are mounting each year is reason enough to justify the belief there is a growing need for top-grade retailing executives. Some of the major shifts that have occurred in retailing are the tremendous growth of suburban stores and shopping centers and the impact of more leisure time and new modes of living on our whole concept of the types of clothing and home furnishings people want. Retail stores move with these changes, and the people who can best anticipate them, who have the imagination to capitalize on them, have unlimited horizons in the business where change is such a vital part of life.

Some authorities believe that the total expenditures of our population will increase by 120 per cent in the next twenty years. The sales of retailers will go right along with the same rate of growth so that by 1975 retail sales in this country may well total $400 billion. Consequently, the future outlook for an interesting and rewarding career in retailing is most attractive.

The very fact the retail sales are going higher year after year points up the growing need for more top grade executives. So it is but natural to find retailing stressing the importance of recruiting better trained, better educated people to its ranks. Stores need the strength and vision, the imagination and enthusiasm that well-educated young people can bring to their ranks. They need people who will fight to find the right answers.

THE RUBBER INDUSTRY

J. Ward Keener
President
B. F. Goodrich Company

The key word for the rubber industry is "diversification." Yet we have not become diversified simply for the sake of getting into a myriad of products and industrial areas. All of our diversification has stemmed from logically planned research approaches, backed with technical and production capabilities.

Our products range through the rubber, petrochemical, and chemical fields. They have largely come from basic rubber research and polymer know-how. From the experiments in our research laboratories we have developed manufacturing facilities for products ranging from rubber materials and rubber goods through synthetic fibers and rigid vinyl materials.

As our national standards of living increase, normally the rubber products business experiences a corresponding annual growth. However, the most dramatic growth potentials lie in our petrochemical and chemical fields. The opportunities ahead in rigid plastic vinyls for use in the structural industries, for example, are great.

Career opportunities are as diversified as imagination will allow. The chemist, the physicist, the engineer—each has exciting challenges before him. But, naturally, our growth will require much more than research specialists. We must have marketing, production, financial, employee relations, and other specialized people in order to get our products into the hands of the consumer. And, though the opportunities are great for specialists of all kinds, they are even greater for individuals with flexibility and broad perspectives who are capable of becoming outstanding generalists—for it is only through the leadership and coordinating abilities of the generalists that the specialists can make their fullest contributions.

THE STEEL INDUSTRY

C. F. Hood
President
United States Steel Corporation

America is a great and growing land. The energy and resourcefulness of the engineer and the scientist, using new knowledge of physical forces and the natural elements, have created new forms of energy and mechanical processes, new man-made materials and wonders of design and construction.

As members of a basic industry, therefore, the steel companies of America face a long list of tremendous and challenging potentialities. Despite the past progress of which all of us are so justly proud, the steel industry in these United States may well be only in its infancy. Even now, our research people are years ahead in their efforts to anticipate the needs and the promise of tomorrow. Our engineers have the task of designing equipment and processes which can make tomorrow's steels commercial realities. Our chemists are using coal chemicals to forge new links in the long chain of modern synthetic materials. And, day by day, people of many talents in the steel industry strive to reach new heights in satisfying human aspirations by giving added strength to the bases of better human relationships.

Accurate predictions of the future are not within the scope of mortal ability, but there is one thing of which I am certain. The steel industry can meet any challenge so long as it continues to have the services of young men and women who can help to open up new and broader vistas by contributing their talents and imaginations to the constant progress being made in the age old art of making steel.

America is the product of free and self-governed people working together, earning their separate ways, adhering to fundamental laws of economic achievement and moral improvement. No one can tell the young person of today what he or she can or should do in the promising array of opportunities before us. It remains for the individual to make up his own mind. The important thing is to set a goal, chart a course, then do the best one can. In an atmosphere of freedom and individual growth, personal ability and effort will always be the essential elements of personal success.

PUBLIC UTILITIES

J. THEODORE WOLFE
President, *Baltimore Gas and Electric Company*
President, *American Gas Association*

To many people, obsessed with the notion that only those fields which are new can be fertile, it may come as a surprise to learn that three of America's largest and oldest enterprises are among the most rapidly growing. These are the three branches of the public utility industry—electricity, gas, and telephone. Doubling in size every ten years or less, each of them offers unlimited opportunity to the young man planning a lifetime career.

My concept of a satisfying career is one which affords me pride in the job I am doing, which offers me the opportunity to advance on merit, which gives me a feeling of belonging to the community in which I work, which surrounds me with an atmosphere of friendliness, which assures me adequate and fair compensation, which provides me with economic security for the protection of my family, and which recognizes my desire to be treated, and to treat each of the people with whom I work, as an individual human being. All of these conditions are present to a marked degree in the public utility industry.

Opportunities for employment in the utility industry are many and varied. The desire of Americans for higher and higher living standards creates an ever-growing demand for electric, gas, and telephone service. Only through the combined efforts of engineers, accountants, administrators, salesmen, research specialists, and people in countless other capacities can this demand be met with timeliness and with efficiency. There is a challenge here for each of us.

CHAPTER TEN

OPPORTUNITIES IN EDUCATION

For years now, the education field has enjoyed a universally bad press. And, strangely enough, it is the friends of education who have been largely responsible for the tons of adverse publicity that have filled the newspapers and the magazines in the years since the end of World War II.

Economic Prospects

The great bulk of this bad publicity has been generated in an attempt to obtain better salaries for teachers. To a large measure, this campaign has been effective. While teachers' salaries are still not all that they should be, the general public has been alerted to the problem and many communities are moving steadily and surely to see that their teachers receive a salary commensurate with the responsibilities of their position. In two states, New York and California, the salary scale for public school teachers has already reached a point where it compares favorably with many other occupations.

But fifteen years of intensive publicity about the poor, underpaid teacher has had its effect on the number and the calibre of the young men and women entering the teaching profession. It is no secret that there is a shortage of teachers in almost every public school system in the nation. It is less well known, but just as true, that the young men and women studying to become teachers represent the poorest students now in college.

This is only natural. The ambitious, energetic, intelligent student has been told, ever since he can remember, that the teaching profession was a certain road to poverty. It is little wonder that the better, more alert students looked for opportunities in the new and expanding and well-paying occupations, such as advertising and electrical engineering.

It is true that there have always been bright students who wanted to teach. The cold, hard facts of economics have not deterred them, and the field of education is richer today for their sacrifice. But sacrifice should not be necessary. Teaching, they say, has its own reward. But, the great mass of young people in search of a career must temper their enthusiasm for their chosen profession with a realistic evaluation of the crassly commercial rewards offered by that profession.

After years of headlines explaining that school teachers are paid less than garbage collectors, it is very difficult to approach the subject of teachers' salaries with an open mind. However, the young man or woman now in college who has toyed with the concept of teaching as a career would be wise not to reject the idea without a full study of salary conditions in his or her area at the present time. Teacher salaries are being raised every year, and what was true when the student was a freshman may not be true as the student approaches graduation.

This is not to say that the teaching profession is now one of the better paying occupations. It does mean that the public school teacher is now paid more than he was five years ago, and there is every reason to believe that this trend will continue.

The Expansion of Education

If the expansion of any industry means an increase in the number of opportunities available within that industry, then education within the next few years will offer more opportunities than can be counted. And there is nothing problematical about the expansion of education. This is not an industry in the drawing board stage. Education must be geared to the millions of children now alive who must, by law, be exposed to at least ten years of formal schooling.

The *Rockefeller Report on Education* reports that by 1975 there will be almost 42 million Americans between the ages of five and fourteen. These are the children who must be sent to school. If it is assumed that the ideal figure of thirty children to a classroom is obtained, 1,400,000 teachers will be required at the kindergarten, elementary, and junior-high levels alone.

By 1969 the public high schools will be facing a student enrollment 50 to 70 per cent greater than it is at the present time. By 1975 the colleges and universities will double or triple their present enrollments. At the present time there are 150,000 institutions of learning in the United States, and more schools are under construction every day.

Of course, this boom in education means that there are going to be many more jobs for teachers. It also means that there are going to be many more opportunities for teachers to advance to supervisory posts within the various school systems. More schools mean more principals and assistant principals, more counselors and subject supervisors. Bigger school systems are going to require more staff people to prepare curricula, to organize new courses, and to carry out the everyday administrative functions of a big business organization.

Advancement in Education

The superintendent of a large city school system can earn as much as $42,000. A high-school principal in a metropolitan area can earn from between $12,000 and $15,000. These figures, of course, do not compare with the salaries that industry pays for men of comparable ability, but it does indicate that there are posts in education that pay better than manual labor.

The classroom teacher is the building block of our educational system. And because he is so important, all of the emphasis on poor salaries has been centered on the plight of this man.

The young man or the young woman who chooses teaching as a lifetime career quite often expects to spend the rest of his or her life in the classroom. This is a situation that is unknown in other professions. The young engineer may enter industry as little more than a draftsman, but he does not expect to spend the rest of his life on the drafting table.

He expects to become a group leader, a section chief, a department head, a member of the management team of the corporation that has hired him. The same is true of the business administration student with an accounting background. He begins his career by doing bookkeeping work, but he has no desire to be chained to the adding machine for the rest of his life. He, too, looks for a series of promotions that will reward him with more responsibilities and more money.

In the past, school systems have been rather static. There has been little opportunity for the classroom teacher to move upward to better paying positions. However, the great expansion of all educational systems that must take place in the next ten to twenty years will make it possible for many more classroom teachers to find better posts within the public school systems.

Educational Requirements

When this opportunity for advancement is coupled to a general improvement of the attitude of the public toward educational salaries, the entire education professional picture becomes much brighter than it has appeared for the past decade.

The college senior in the teacher's college has already made his career choice. He knows that he is going to enter education, and his curriculum has been prepared in order that he will have the proper number of education courses required by the public school system in the area in which he wishes to teach. The college senior in a liberal arts college who decides that he would like to teach in a public school system will find that even with his A.B. degree, he is at a slight disadvantage. His local school system may grant him a temporary teaching certificate, but he will pay a penalty in salary, and he must promise to take the required twelve or fifteen hours of "education" courses that are needed for full certification. If the liberal arts student is fortunate enough to be able to make the decision to enter teaching at the end of his junior year, a few summer courses and a heavy course load in his senior year may make it possible for him to qualify at graduation for a full teaching assignment.

The teaching profession is no place for the young man who doesn't like to go to school. Once in teaching, the new member of the profession will soon learn that future salary increases are closely tied to graduate school work. So many credit hours of work in graduate school are worth $200 or $300 a year in salary. And, should the young teacher be advanced to a supervisory post, he will find it just as important—if not more so—that he go on with his advanced studies. The upper echelon posts in education are filled almost exclusively by men and women with M.A. and Ph.D. degrees in Education. Recently, the state of New York appointed a new man to its top public education supervisory post. The fact that this man did not have an advanced degree in education was the subject of a long article in the *New York Times*—so rare have such appointments become.

Private Schools

The college senior who decides to make a career of teaching in one of the nation's private schools faces a different set of problems than does his public school counterpart. On the critical wage question, the private school teacher will discover that in many cases his pay check is even less than that of the public school teacher. This lower paycheck is sometimes offset by subsidiary benefits, such as school-provided housing and meals in the student dining hall.

Because a private school is not part of a large administrative organization, there are corresponding less opportunities for advancement to supervisory and administrative posts. Advancement for the teacher in the private school must usually wait upon a vacancy appearing in the administration of his school. It is also common for a teacher to change schools in search of a better position. However, private schools, like all other phases of education, are experiencing a period of growth and expansion. There are more jobs in the private school field then ever before, and this is a situation that can only continue.

But the private school does offer a number of advantages that the public school system cannot hope to match. The great majority of these advantages are in terms of personal satisfaction. For example, the private school makes it possible for the new teacher to enter his profession without taking the usual run of education courses. The result of this lack of entrance requirements is that the A.B. student is able to step directly from the graduation platform into a teaching position in a private school. The private schools are also able to permit the teacher far more latitude in the planning of his work than is possible in the public school systems with their city and county-wide programs.

The young man who signs a contract to teach in a private school also has the advantage of choosing the school in which he is to teach. The public school teacher whose contract is with a city or a county may find himself assigned anywhere from the slums to the best residential area. Because private schools generally attract students from better income groups, the private school teacher may avoid the serious disciplinary problems that sometimes beset the public school teacher.

It is because of these factors that the private school is able to offer lower salaries than those of the public school system. However, the teacher in the private school need not starve to death. Because of the longer summer vacations and the absence of the need to continually accumulate graduate degree credits, the private school teacher is in a much better position to supplement his teaching pay with summer employment. And because most private school students are serious about entering college, extra money can be obtained by tutoring students.

A Word of Warning

Make no mistake, neither the private nor the public school teacher is going to become rich at his profession, but the salaries available are generally a bit better than that of the much publicized garbage collector. However, one word of warning is in order. The salaries offered by various states and even for the counties and the towns within those states can vary considerably. The college senior who is considering teaching as a career should carefully check into the pay scales in the area in which he wishes to teach. If geographic considerations are no problem, then the student can pick the school system that offers the most money.

However, if a student wishes to teach school in his own home town, he may find that the comparison with the garbage collector is really not too far out of line. It is something worth checking into.

Colleges and Universities

It is difficult enough to discuss teaching salaries in the public and private school systems, so varied is the range offered in different areas. But it is next to impossible to discuss the salary situation in the nation's colleges and universities. A full professor in one of the big, famous eastern universities may earn as much as $20,000 a year with an additional income derived from his writing and outside lecturing. A full professor in a small southern, mountain college may earn less than $5,000 a year and be saddled with a teaching load so heavy that he has little time for outside writing or speaking.

It is even impossible to generalize about the big state universities. Some offer salaries that compare with any college or university in the country while others are much lower on the scale.

Obviously, it would be foolish to recommend that a young man prepare himself to become a college professor in a poor school that offers very low wages. While it is true that in such a post he would be able to provide real help to the students of the college, it is doubtful as to how much help he would be to himself.

It is evident that the nation, as a whole, must do something and do it quickly to make it possible for the many small colleges of the country to pay a living wage to their teaching staff. But the solution does not lie in advising bright, eager, and alert young people to continue to accept such poor salaries.

To clarify the situation, this section will treat the opportunities in college teaching as they are related to the top fifty or seventy-five colleges and universities in the United States. Perhaps the first distinction to be made is that between the college and the university. The young man who sincerely wants to teach had best chart a course toward one of the better colleges. Here, teaching will be his prime responsibility, and his advancement will be based largely upon how well he is able to train his students. In the universities, another set of criteria prevails. The professor is still expected to teach—but not as much or as often as the college professor—and he is expected to continue to perform the same kind of original research that earned him his Ph.D. "Publish or Perish" is the unwritten code of the university, and the young man whose natural bent is for classroom teaching rather than scholarly research will find a much happier climate on the small college campus.

The small college is also likely to lay less stress on the Ph.D., although the American passion for advanced degrees has reached into the small schools and this is no longer as true as it once was. At the university, the Ph.D. is essential for advancement to the full professorship. Only in rare cases is a man with an A.B. or even a M.A. advanced to full professorial rank.

In the years to come, the young man just starting out in college teaching may find his greatest opportunities in the large state universities. The big private schools are not in a position to greatly enlarge their student bodies, but the state schools are politically committed to absorb the rush of students who are most assuredly on their way to the ivy halls of higher education. The University of California, for example, predicts that it will have 90,000 students by 1975. The need for department heads, assistant department heads, and deans in an organization of that size is obvious.

In some of the smaller institutions, such as Johns Hopkins, the administration is committed to a policy of maintaining approximately its present size and admitting only the best students available. These schools hope to be able to attract professors by providing them with top-notch, talented students rather than through the promise of rapid promotion because of a greatly increased student body.

The student who chooses college teaching as a career must plan on going to graduate school at least long enough to get a Master's degree. Here the university has some advantage over the college. Most universities make provision for an "on the job training program" that enables the student to earn a small salary as a junior instructor while studying for his advanced degree. It is also often possible for a young man to serve as an assistant professor while earning credits toward his Ph.D.

The early years in the college or university teacher's life are not well-paying ones. Even in the schools that offer good salaries to full professors, the lower teaching ranks are not paid too well. This is a situation that is slowly being corrected, but it means that the young man, fresh out of graduate school, will still have a few lean years before his salary reaches anything like a satisfactory level.

For students who wish to teach the sciences in the university, the future is a little brighter. Two events have transpired to raise the income of the university science professor. The first is the demand by industry for top scientists, and, because industry has been willing to pay good wages to its better technical people, the universities have been forced to make corresponding salary increases in order to retain their teaching staff. Salaries are still not equal to that of industry, but on almost any university campus the full professor of English will earn less money than his counterpart in the physics

department. The second event that has increased the opportunities
for the science teacher has been the introduction of large amounts
of government-sponsored research on the campus. These government contracts have enabled the university to pay the professor an
extra salary for work which in the past would have been considered
to be part of his professorial duties.

But the rewards of college teaching are not all monetary. If they
were, the nation's higher education system would have collapsed
years ago. Young men go into college teaching because they really
and truly want that kind of life. It is a fortunate circumstance that
the chances of their obtaining better wages and more opportunities
for advancement in the years ahead are better than they have been
for some time.

On any college campus, there are many opportunities outside of
the classroom and the research laboratories. Universities are big
business with all of the administrative problems that go with big
business. They have need of business managers, public relations
men, accountants, plant managers, and general administrators. A
progressive university also maintains a squad of secondary school
recruiters similar to the college recruiter who has figured so
prominently in this book.

The positions that make up the administrative staff of a university
are similar to corresponding positions in industry. As a general rule,
the salaries are a notch below the standard prevailing industrial
rate, but this is usually more than made up by the "academic in-
tangibles" and a working atmosphere that is generally far less demanding than that of a downtown office building or a factory.

Opportunities in Government

Education in America is big business. There is no other way to
describe it. In terms of people employed, people served, physical
plant, and impact on the community, it is just plain Big. And anything that grows to this size simply has to come in contact with the
Federal Government. The Department of Health, Education and
Welfare employs large numbers of administrative people with an
educational background and uses people trained in educational research techniques to constantly study and evaluate the nation's educational systems.

Educational Associations

And just as business has the National Association of Manufacturers and its chambers of commerce, the educational field has a whole host of organizations designed to serve its various groups. The National Education Association is perhaps the largest of these groups but others are designed to serve college public-relations men, elementary school teachers, teachers colleges, and college professors; there is even an association for nonaccredited colleges. All of these do important work in furthering the interests of their members and are staffed primarily by people who have had some educational experience. They are heavy on public relations techniques and often publish large numbers of reports, magazines, and booklets for the guidance of their membership.

In terms of salaries offered, they compare favorably with commercial trade organizations at all levels except those at the top of the bigger trade groups. Some of the better positions in the educational field exist in these peripheral organizations.

The Future in Education

Perhaps the greatest cross that the people in education have had to bear in the last few decades has been the general public apathy toward education in general and the loss of prestige suffered by the teaching profession in general. While the college professor in this country has never had the respect of the public that is enjoyed by the professor at a European university, there have been times in the history of America when he was considered to be a valued member of any community. The same situation, on a lesser scale was once true of the teaching profession in general.

There is considerable evidence that the attitude of the public is about to change. The shift will not occur overnight. But the general, persistent clamor on all sides to raise both the standards of American education and the salaries of the people in education is certain to make the great bulk of the population more aware of the problems of education. And with this awareness will come a new respect for the people in the field.

Despite the many problems of education and despite the discouraging history of the profession during the past two decades, the young man entering the teaching profession today can do so with full confidence in the future. It is certain that the rewards for teaching can only increase and with the increased monetary return will come a corresponding increase in the status and prestige of the entire teaching profession.

CHAPTER ELEVEN

OPPORTUNITIES IN
GOVERNMENT

7,380,000 JOBS.

7,380,000 people are on the payrolls of the Federal, state, and local governments in the United States. And that figure does not include the men and women in the armed services.

Surprisingly enough, the greatest concentration of these jobs is at the local level. Over three million people work for municipal governments from New York to Chula Vista, from Fargo to Loreado. More than two million people work for state governments and the rest—better than two million—are employed by the Federal government.

In any organization of this size and scope there are certain to be opportunities for many young men with a college background. And these opportunities do exist in all areas and in almost all professions. With the single possible exception of the ministry, the governmental agencies of the United States, the forty-eight states, and thousands of cities and towns employ all types of people from archivists to zoologists.

It is true that government also employs millions of nonprofessional people to do routine chores. Clerks, typists, street cleaners, mailmen, trash collectors, and sewage plant workers make up part of the government payrolls. Policemen and firemen and the teachers in the many local public school systems account for large segments of state and local government employment figures. But, even after all these people have been subtracted from the total 7,380,000 figure, there are still a great many interesting and, sometimes exciting, jobs with government.

The Federal Government

It is within the Federal government that the greatest number of "professional" government positions exist. In the State Department, in the Foreign Service, in the U.S. Information Agency, in the National Security Administration, in the Commerce, Agriculture, and Treasury Departments the Federal government employs historians, economists, foresters, translators, scientists, engineers, radio announcers, writers, agronomists, archivists, biologists, doctors, lawyers, social workers, and cultural relations experts.

In fact, the Federal government is sometimes the only place that offers employment to a neophyte in a specific field. For example, the college senior with a major in political science can find no spot in industry that will utilize him as a political scientist. However, within the National Security Administration of the Federal government he can be assigned to a research project studying the political trends of some foreign country. In another case, the Commerce Department will employ a college graduate with a political economy background and assign him to a project studying the economics of some American industry.

In many fields within the humanities, the Federal government is virtually the only employer outside the university. This does not mean that the political science student or the political economy student cannot find a good job in industry. It simply means that industry is not looking for these men to work at their speciality. These students, upon entering industry, will be trained to become staff assistants and administrators where specific knowledge of the local politics of Bulgaria or the fiscal policies of South Korea will not have direct application.

And, strangely enough, the chances are that industry will pay higher wages to these men than will the government. Yet the government has direct need of the specific training that these men have received in college.

It is almost a truism that working for the government does not pay as well as working for industry and business. And, in many circles, people who work for the government are looked down upon as inferiors who are unable or unwilling to go into industry and work for honest wages. There is just enough truth in this statement for it to be widely accepted as gospel. This attitude often deters a young man from investigating the opportunities in government. No young man wants to work for a poor salary or to be branded as lazy and afraid of hard work. However, in failing to even check into the possibility of a career in government, the young man may be missing a real chance to follow the career he selected as a student.

Advantages

Why should a young man select services with the Federal government as a career?

There are many reasons. Some of them are as mundane as the fact that the Federal government is most generous with such things as sick leave, vacations, health benefits, and pensions. Others are as exciting as the fact that many government agencies have overseas operations and need young men to serve in the jungles of Burma, the mountains of India, and the capitals of Europe.

Government agencies are big, and the man who advances to the position of department chief may have a scope of authority and responsibility that far outstrips that of the president of many industrial concerns. It is true that his salary—perhaps $15,000 a year —will not match that of his industrial counterpart, but the government career worker may have more prestige and more influence.

There is also real satisfaction to be gained from working on projects of national and international significance. For many people, knowing the inside story behind a revolution in South America can be more exciting than knowing the inside story behind the launching of a new line of cosmetics in the nation's drugstores. For these people, a copy of Paris *Match* is much more interesting than the *Wall Street Journal*.

To the Federal government employee stationed in Washington, there is the added zest of being a part of a world capital. There is always a sense of participation in world affairs—no matter how routine or insignificant the individual's own particular job may be. This is a feeling that cannot be gained by working for a manufacturer of hardware products in the Midwest.

Still another reason for entering the service of the Federal government lies in the emphasis that the Federal agencies place on training and education. Nearly every government department has extensive training programs for new employees, and many offer in-service training institutes for men and women who have been with the agency for a given period of time. Sometimes this training takes the form of one or two classes a day with the rest of the employee's time spent on the job. In other cases, the training consists of full time schooling with a full day's schedule of classes and homework to be done in the evening.

Training courses are becoming common in industry. But in government they are almost universal. One reason for this, perhaps, is because industry is still somewhat reluctant to spend large sums of money to train employees who, one day, may go to work for a competitor. The government has no direct competitor, and should a man trained by the Treasury Department transfer to the Department of Commerce, the government has not lost the training dollars it has invested in the man.

Another great lure of government employment is the security that it offers. While the government has been known to cut back its employment rolls, such action is rare enough to make it the subject of headlines in newspapers across the country. The Civil Service Commission also exists to protect the individual worker against injustices. The Civil Service Commission is not a union, but its function is to look after the welfare of all government workers. Few professional employees in industry have similar protection.

Disadvantages

These, then, are the advantages of a career in government service. What are the disadvantages?

It has already been indicated that salaries in government positions often do not compare with those paid for similar posts in industry. This is particularly true in the higher administrative positions. At the lower levels, particularly at the grades open to beginners in government service, salaries compare favorably with those offered elsewhere.

It is sometimes difficult for a man who has spent eight or ten years in government service to find a comparable job in industry, should he tire of his government assignment. Right or wrong, industry has developed an inbred distrust of government workers.

This is not always warranted, but the attitude persists and makes it difficult for men to leave government service.

Industry does hire people from government agencies, but it makes its selections with great care. Top level departmental administrators can usually make the switch from government to industry and greatly improve their salary status in the process. Defense industries often hire men from government procurement agencies because of the knowledge that these men have of the massive government paperwork procedures.

It is at the governmental staff level that men seeking the switch to industry suffer the greatest disappointments. A good, efficient, hard-working staff assistant to the top man in a government agency may be earning $12,000. He knows that his counterpart in industry is earning $20,000, yet he is unable to enter industry because of the popular notion that government agencies are over-staffed with men who spend their time compiling useless reports on obscure subjects.

In the top secret agencies, such as the National Security Administration or the Central Intelligence Agency, another factor works against the man attempting to move from government to industry. Because of security regulations, he is not allowed to discuss his past work with anyone. All that can be said by such an individual is that he was a GS-11 (Government Service Salary Grade No. 11) and that he resigned. Should a prospective employer write to the personnel office of one of these agencies, for information on the employee, he will be given the same meager data.

From this it is obvious that the decision to work for these government agencies should not be made lightly. And it is all the more important because both NSA and CIA make extensive use of the college recruiter and, at the same time, offer some of the most attractive assignments in government service. The lure of a good assignment, a post in Washington, the glamor of the cloak and dagger atmosphere, and the choice of a wide variety of training programs can be a heady wine to the college senior. The problem for the young man is complicated by the fact that the recruiter can say very little about the type of work being done by his agency. The result of all this mystery is that young men stay with these agencies either for one or two years, or for life. There is no middle ground.

Specialized Areas

The senior in a liberal arts college, who has discovered that he has a natural bent for foreign languages, has a serious employment problem. He can, of course, go into teaching, but that means more schooling and perhaps he has neither the money nor the inclination to continue his university training. There are a few jobs in companies with overseas commitments, but that field is limited. For this man, government service holds real promise. The Army, Navy, Air Force, State Department, National Security Administration, the Central Intelligence Agency, and other agencies have standing requirements for translators.

For the rare student who finds his niche in library work or, better yet, in the more specialized area of archives, the government offers virtually the only outlet for his talents. Few university or municipal libraries are large enough to employ archivists. The Federal government has hundreds. And some state governments also employ people with these skills.

While industry generally underrates government workers, there are some areas where government work represents the highest degree of professional competence. The United States Coast and Geodetic Survey employs top geologists and cartographers. Needless to say, top men from this agency can find employment in industry. Only in the petroleum and mining industries can geologists find equivalent employment, and, even in these cases, the work may be too specialized to appeal to the individual student.

A similar situation exists in the forestry section of the Department of the Interior. Paper companies with their own stands of timber and logging outfits have respect for the experienced government forester.

Science and Engineering

But these are specialized occupations. What of the more common professions? In science and engineering government service offers a number of advantages. While pay, especially in the lower grades is not up to industry standards, advancement can be more rapid. At the higher salary levels government engineers and scientists fare as well or better than the average engineer in, for example, a large airframe company. Another advantage of government assignments in this field lies in the fact that many government laboratories are extremely well equipped. Installations such as the David Taylor Model Basin and the Naval Research Laboratory have few equivalents in industry. In the nuclear field, the Atomic Energy Commission still maintains almost a monopoly in basic research facilities.

Medicine

It is difficult to generalize about any professions within government. The Federal government is so big; it employs so many people in so many different places that no hard and fast rules can be established. Medicine is a good example of this. Many government operated hospitals are perpetually understaffed because of the difficulty of attracting doctors to work for government salaries. Some of these hospitals offer substandard medical care. Yet the National Institutes of Health in Bethesda, Maryland, attracts some of the top medical research people in the country to work, at low salaries, on exciting research projects in a superbly equipped medical facility.

The Historian

Similar situations exist in other fields. The government employs historians. Some of these are assigned to interesting research projects while others are given routine assignments that are both unchallenging and dull. For example, the Air Force assigns a historian to each wing. Should the historian be sent to an air transport wing in the southern part of the United States, his work will be very routine. However, should the assignment be with an overseas SAC base, where the very existence of American forces is a constant source of trouble for American foreign policy, the historian may find himself writing meaningful history.

Investigating the Field

The man who goes to work in industry in his own home town is likely to have a good idea of what his present and future assignments will be. The size of government makes this kind of knowledge very difficult for the college senior to obtain. The young man interested in government service should make every effort to learn all he can about a government agency before he agrees to report to work.

Even the more glamorous aspects of government service, such as the foreign service, can have serious drawbacks. There are only so many posts in Paris and London, and there are a great many assignments in remote towns in Burma, Ceylon, Chile, Ethiopia, and India. In recent years, the government has made a serious attempt to attract better personnel for foreign service work, and it now offers a number of advantages in terms of advanced schooling and rotating assignments. For the man who wants to see the world the foreign service offers opportunities available nowhere else. It should be pointed out that the foreign service, while part of the Department of State, is not concerned with high diplomacy. The foreign service officer is assigned to look after the interests of American citizens and American business in foreign countries. He is concerned with such things as visas, passports, trade permits, immigration quotas, and stranded tourists. The requirements for entering the foreign service are not as rigid as for some of the career posts in the diplomatic sections of the State Department.

Positions with the State Department are usually highly prized and have great prestige value within government service. These positions can quite often lead to ambassadorial rank. The wealthy man who becomes a politically appointed ambassador is slowly going out of style, and more and more posts are going to long-term career men with the State Department.

Government is such a sprawling mass of agencies that there is literally a career for everyone. Do you want to be a writer or a radio announcer? The U.S. Information Agency can use you. The pay is less than Time magazine or NBC, but it is often better than a small town newspaper or radio station and there are no advertisers who must be pleased. There are, however, severe critics on Capitol Hill who must be satisfied.

Do you want to be a civil engineer? The U.S. Army Engineers build more dams, bridges, and harbors than any construction firm in the world, and they do much of it with civilian employees.

Do you want to be a geographer or a demographer? Try the Department of the Interior or the Census Bureau.

The list is almost endless. Your local Post Office can furnish you with full data on many of the opportunities in government. And your Congressman will be most happy to have someone in his office track down all the literature on the jobs available in any field. Nothing pleases a Congressman more than to be able to find a job for one of his constituents.

Advancement

One final word of caution. There are a great many positions in every government agency for people with less than a college education. Before accepting a position with the government, the young man should make certain that he is taking a post that requires all of the qualifications that he possesses. Promotions and salary increases in government service are often based on length of service. Acceptance of a job at a grade level below his full qualifications could cost the young man as much as two years of his career. Care in selecting his first post can prevent this wasted time.

Although promotions are often based on length of service, the government does not discriminate against the man with talent and energy. Supervisors in government agencies are no less alert to good personnel than their counterparts in industry. Good people are promoted in the government every day. Of course, some mediocre people are also promoted each day simply because they have held their past jobs for a given length of time. However, the better man will move at a much faster pace.

All of the criticism of government workers is not completely unfounded. There are a great many people on the government payrolls who would have great difficulty earning a living in industry. However, it is for this very reason that the man with initiative and drive can make a mark in government service.

State Government

Thus far, all of the discussion has centered on employment opportunities with the Federal government. The state government also offers a number of positions to college-trained people. But, usually, the state equivalent of Federal jobs is less attractive on both an assignment and a salary basis.

While there are as many positions in state governments as exist in the Federal government, there are fewer opportunities for the college-trained man seeking employment in a specialized field. States do hire college-trained men for administrative posts, but there is little of the recruiting that is done by the Federal agencies. Civil engineers are required by the States Roads Commission, but the big research facilities of the Navy, the Atomic Energy Commission, Health, Education and Welfare, or the Air Force do not exist at the state level.

Many of the professional functions of the Departments of Commerce, Interior, or Agriculture also exist at the state level but on a reduced scale. Often these tasks are performed as an adjunct of the state university.

And, almost invariably, the wage scale at the state level is lower than that of the Federal government.

However, there are advantages to working for the state government. Not the least is the opportunity to work in your own locality. Not everyone wants to live in Washington, and certainly there are large numbers of people for whom the jungles of Burma hold no appeal.

There are also advantages to working in a smaller organization. Many people will feel lost in a government agency where there are 7,000 workers in the same office building. The state Civil Service positions usually offer the same fringe benefits in terms of vacations, sick leave, and pensions as do the Federal government, and these benefits may be better than those available in the local industry.

It is often possible for a state employee to combine his state job with some outside activity. If the position is not a particularly demanding one—and there are more of these at the state level than at the Federal—a young man might take on some sideline such as insurance or real estate.

At the present time, state governments have not felt it necessary to recruit or to train vast numbers of college people for their Civil Service posts. However, this will change. As the population increases, the number of people on the state payrolls will increase. And with the resulting complexity of state government will come a demand for more highly qualified personnel to man the state agencies.

This time is not yet with us, and the young man inquiring about a position with a state agency should carefully evaluate the opportunities available to him in that position. He should then weigh these opportunities against those open to him in the Federal government and in industry before making a final choice.

Local Government

The great variety of cities, towns, and villages that make up the United States makes it impossible to discuss opportunities available in municipal governments. More people work for cities and towns than for either the Federal government or for the governments of the forty-eight states.

A city such as New York will have a Civil Service payroll greater than that of many states. In a small village the municipal payroll may consist of the mayor, his brothers, and his two nephews. Obviously, it is impossible to advise a course of action to anyone in the face of such diversity.

However, it can be said that the great bulk of the more than three million jobs available with local governments are filled by personnel with less than college training. Certainly, it is a field that does not actively recruit college seniors.

City government requires the services of large numbers of social workers and recreation directors. These people are usually college trained. It is unfortunate that the salary scale paid to these important people is quite often geared to the wage scale of other municipal employees.

There are, however, other areas of municipal administration that deserve consideration by the college student. More and more cities and towns are adapting the city manager form of government. These men are highly trained administrators, and several colleges are currently offering both undergraduate and graduate work designed to equip a man to fill such a post.

Other specialized jobs, such as city planning and traffic control, demand men with college training. However, unless the college senior has decided upon such a career before his senior year, he is not likely to be in a position to qualify for a post of this kind.

Politics quite often enter into the distribution of positions with a city government to a degree that is not possible in the state and Federal systems protected by Civil Service regulations. The young man considering a career in city affairs is in a far better position to judge his own political connection than is any outsider.

It is impossible to frame a general statement about government service. There are good positions and there are dull, routine, low-paying jobs that should be avoided at all costs. It is an area that should be approached with caution by the college senior. Because of the variety of opportunities that do exist, it is a field well worth serious consideration. But each position should be carefully considered on its own merits. Because the man in the next block has a good post in the government is no guarantee that any government job will be equally good.

Unlike industry, where a given company can earn a reputation for being a good place in which to work, the same Federal government agency can offer both good and bad positions. But the necessity of a cautious approach to government service should not discourage the college senior. By arbitrarily dismissing a career in government, he may be passing up an opportunity for a fine career in the profession of his choice.

CHAPTER TWELVE

OPPORTUNITIES IN THE PROFESSIONS

The Doctor

From *Arrowsmith* to *Young Doctor Malone,* from *Men in White* to *Yellow Jack,* the American doctor has been a recurring theme in the nation's literature. The American doctor has been pictured as a kindly old philosopher working tirelessly through long snowy nights to deliver babies and to set broken legs of old farmers. He has also been pictured as a cold, aloof, and brilliant specialist working in the glare of the lights of the operating room. Even when novelists have attempted an unflattering portrait of the doctor, the picture is painted more with tragedy than with malice.

The doctor is not only a popular figure in literature, he is a popular figure in motion pictures, on the stage, and in the daily soap operas. The latter medium has turned the men in white into something resembling folk heroes. Ministers, priests, and rabbis enjoy a high level of prestige, but their appeal is limited to followers of their faith. The appeal of the doctor is universal.

Why?

There are probably two reasons—the first, emotional, and the second, rational. The emotional reason, of course, is that the doctor deals daily with life and death, and men still hold in awe other men whose work involves the secret of life. The second reason—the rational one—is that every layman realizes that the road to becoming a doctor is long and hard; one that involves a great deal of work and a great deal of sacrifice. The college senior who has plans of becoming a doctor has been told this many times, but it is something that bears repeating.

The first hurdle for the college senior is to find some medical school that will accept him for the necessary four years of graduate study that lead to the M.D. degree. This, in itself, is no small task. Most medical schools are small and are likely to remain so because of the staggering cost of educating a medical student. At Johns Hopkins, for example, the tuition in the medical school is $1,200 a year, and the cost to the university of educating that student is almost nine times the tuition figure. If the cost of a medical education is high to the student, then the cost to the university is enormous. This is one of the major reasons for the very strict admission policy of all medical schools.

The college senior looking about for a medical school should keep in mind a number of factors. The first is that within recent years a number of medical schools have made strenuous and successful efforts to improve the quality of their instruction. It is no longer true that there are only two or three medical schools of any worth in the country. There are many.

A second factor to be kept in mind is that it is often advisable for a doctor to obtain his medical education at the school that is most popular in his section of the country. For example, if the majority of doctors in a certain metropolitan area received their training at Harvard, a doctor from the University of Minnesota may find himself an outsider. This clannishness is not limited to Harvard men, for the Harvard graduate in a community of Minnesota trained doctors will feel equally out of place.

If the old school tie is important in the business world, it is doubly important in a closely knit group such as the medical profession. This advice may not hold true for the doctor who wishes to become a research man or for the gifted surgeon who needs the guidance of the leading specialist in his field, but it is good advice for the general practitioner.

The college senior going into medicine can look forward to four more years of schooling and at least one, probably two, years of internship. Then, at the end of all this training, he is very likely to have to serve two years in one of the armed services as a doctor. If the college senior is twenty-one or twenty-two years old at graduation, he will be twenty-nine or thirty before he will actually be ready to set up his office and accept patients.

This represents a sizeable portion of any man's life, and statistics show that doctors have a shorter life span than the general run of the population. There are moves afoot to shorten the training period for doctors. Johns Hopkins is inaugurating a plan which will cut two years from the doctor's total schooling by telescoping the undergraduate and graduate programs and lengthening the school year. This program, if successful, will almost certainly be copied by other medical schools. But, while the Hopkins plan will shorten the number of years of required study, the intensified program can only add to the burden carried by the student during the years that he does spend in school.

The studies leading to the M.D. degree are difficult, and the young man who does not have a burning interest in medicine will not make the grade. The annual income figure of the average doctor is an impressive bit of statistical information, but it can seem far off in the future to the twenty-five year old medical student bogged down in a heavy study program, a schedule of minor hospital duties, and a debt incurred by borrowing funds to pay the expenses of his training.

Even after graduation and internship, the young doctor does not automatically graduate to the upper income bracket. It takes time to build a practice, and it takes even longer to build a reputation as a specialist. The long hours do not end with the close of formal schooling. A doctor works all kinds of hours, day and night, during his early years of practice, and some of them never do lose the habit of constant work. Nor is the doctor finished with his studies at the end of his school years. Medicine is a dynamic science, and the doctor who does not keep up with his reading will soon find that he is out of touch with the profession.

While the young doctor is slowly building up his practice, he has the additional expense of office rental and the need to purchase equipment for that office. Usually he finds that he is well into his thirties before he begins to earn a good income. It is a long, hard grind.

But the rewards are good. A doctor will earn a very sizeable income in his later years. He will enjoy the respect of the community and, in small or middle-sized towns, he will attain considerable prestige. This is less true in the big metropolitan centers where the captains of industry and finance tend to occupy the top prestige positions in the community, but, even here, the doctor can be assured that he will be happily received by all segments of society.

Yet, despite the monetary and social rewards that are available to doctors, many deliberately choose to enter the far less profitable fields of research and teaching. These dedicated men will not have to suffer any serious privations, for the salary paid by research organizations and medical schools is generally excellent; but it is only a fraction of that which could be made by a doctor with a flourishing practice. To these men, the search for new discoveries in medicine has become the most important thing in life, and most would remain in research work even if the salary scale were drastically reduced.

A practicing doctor is actually an independent businessman with many of the problems that beset the operator of the corner store or gas station. He has tax problems and personnel problems; he must maintain a sizeable stock of supplies; he must comply with city and state laws, and, in short, he must become a combination accountant, bookkeeper, and clerk. This method of operation holds little appeal for some doctors, and they have found their way into other positions with government, industry, and insurance companies. While the government positions are not noted for their exceptional salary scales, there are good posts within industry and excellent ones with insurance companies. A doctor need not go into general practice in order to be assured of a satisfactory position.

The day of the general practitioner is rapidly passing. Specialization has become the rule rather than the exception in the medical profession. The medical student or the young doctor will have ample opportunity to determine his area of specialization.

The college senior entering a medical school can be assured that there will be a place in the profession waiting for him when he finally finishes his internship six years from now. The American population is already short of doctors, and that population is still growing. In spite of the great strides already made in medical research, the pace in this field shows only signs of increasing activity. There are always more problems—and different problems—

to solve. As the population ages, for example, more research effort will be expended upon the degenerative diseases.

At the present time, there are plans to increase moderately the number of doctors trained each year, but there are no plans to increase greatly the number of medical schools in the country. The establishment of such schools is a long and costly process. The beginning medical student can be assured of graduating into a seller's market, and no young man could ask for better job prospects than that.

The allure of the seller's market may start many young men on the road to medicine, but that allure is not enough to see them through the many very difficult years that lie between the A.B. and the end of medical training. A few may go through all the years of hard work simply because they know that there will eventually be a monetary reward, but the vast majority of doctors make the really great sacrifice in time and effort because, for them, there is just no other way of life.

And this is the reason why the general public sometimes makes folk heroes out of the men in white.

The Dentist

In many ways the problems of the young dentist are very similar to those of the young doctor. Both in the number of years of training and in the time required to establish a practice, the medical and dental professions have strong parallels. However, the dentist must do his work without the benefit of folk hero status. There are few novels and no soap operas about gallant dentists, and, within recent times, the Federal Trade Commission has even banished the dentist from the television toothpaste commercial.

The young man who selects dentistry as a career does so because he is genuinely interested in dentistry. While the monetary rewards can be quite attractive, the man without a real interest in his career will soon discover that filling teeth and dealing with nervous and jittery patients can become rather trying on a daily basis. The amount of effort expended by the dental student in learning dentistry is almost equal to that of the medical student. This effort is hardly worth while unless the student has a real desire to learn the detailed knowledge required by the profession.

While some dental schools admit students after two or three years of undergraduate work, more and more universities are demanding an A.B. or a B.S. degree for admittance. There is also a tendency to stretch the three-year dental program into four years. While it is true that the dentist usually does not have an internship to serve, his length of formal study is roughly equivalent to that of the medical student. (At least one state does, however, require an internship.)

The cost of dental education is also high. Not only does the student have to pay the regular tuition fees, but also his equipment costs during his school years are quite likely to run high. The high cost of this equipment is something that will continue to plague the young dentist long after graduation. In setting up his first practice, the new dentist will be forced, quite often, to go rather deeply into debt in order to equip his new office.

Another problem facing the young man graduating from dental school is that of duty in the armed services. This, however, can be quite a blessing in disguise. It can serve effectively as an internship, giving the new dentist an opportunity to solve all types of dental problems—often in the most modern facilities—without the added burden of worrying about how to convince the patient that his discomfort was necessary. Service patients do not require the ultimate in chairside manner.

Dentistry as a career within the armed services has a number of advantages. Not only does the government often supply the best in equipment, but it also offers some excellent postgraduate training in special schools. While it is true that the dentist in private practice can often make more money than his counterpart in the service, he is also quite likely to have to work a great deal harder to obtain this extra income.

The greatest problem facing a young dentist after graduation is that of finding the right community in which to practice. This is something that he should begin to think about almost from the time he enters his graduate training at the university. It takes time and effort to build a practice, and, should the dentist later decide to move, he must laboriously rebuild his practice almost from the beginning.

The vast majority of graduating dentists do go into private practice. There are opportunities in specialization, but specialization is only possible within the large population centers. There is a tendency for dentistry to become more specialized than was the case ten or twenty years ago, but the general dentist is still the rule rather than the exception.

The graduating dentist does not have the same range of opportunities open to him that are available to the graduate doctor. For example, research in dentistry does not exist on anything like the scale that it exists within medicine. There is a serious shortage of teachers within the dental colleges, but the pay for this work is much inferior to that afforded through private practice. One of the present drawbacks to the establishment of dental schools at the present time is the shortage of qualified teachers to staff them.

And there is a serious shortage of dentists. More are needed in many areas. In some sections of the country the shortage borders on the "desperate." It is true that the shortage is most acute in areas where the population has shown a notable lack of enthusiasm for supporting a practicing dentist, but, even within the densely populated, higher income communities, there are still excellent opportunities for a dentist.

Like the doctor, the dentist is in his late twenties before he is even ready to begin a practice. And, like the doctor, it will be some years before his income reaches a satisfactory level. Even after he leaves school, the dentist is faced with long hours and hard work. It is not a career for the lazy man seeking an easy fortune. And it is certainly no career for a man who is not genuinely interested in dentistry.

The Lawyer

Occasionally, a successful businessman, in a moment of depression over some complex point of law, will wring his hands and declare boldly, "Every businessman should go to law school!" While this advice is not always practical for the young man about to make his mark in the world, there is more than a little truth in it.

The demand within industry for trained lawyers is great. They are needed for contract negotiations, tax problems, property administration; to settle compensation claims and to help prepare union contracts.

In today's business world, where companies are bought and sold, merged and created almost every day, the lawyer has become an indispensible man. And, from the time of the American Revolution, the lawyer has been a key figure in American politics.

Even if there were no need for lawyers to appear in a court of law, there would be sufficient demand for their services to warrant a young man considering the law as a career. And, of course, lawyers do appear in a court of law. American society has not reached that state of perfection where it can dispense with judges, juries, and lawyers.

The traditional route into law has been as a law clerk in the office of an established law firm. Only a few years ago, the wages paid to a law clerk were equivalent to carfare and lunch money. This situation has improved somewhat, but a really good law firm still considers it quite a privilege for a young man to be hired by the firm at all. Salary is definitely a secondary consideration. And these good law firms are correct. This is the best training that a young lawyer could have. Perhaps the best thing that could happen to a law student would be to obtain summer employment with such a firm prior to graduation. But assignments like this are difficult to obtain in spite of the poor salary offered.

A young lawyer advances slowly through a law firm until, somewhere between the age of thirty-five and forty-five, he is made a partner in the firm. If, for any number of reasons, this does not come about, the lawyer strikes out on his own or resigns himself to being a career lawyer. A third alternative and, not necessarily a last resort by any means, would be a post within industry.

A great many of the young men who graduate from law school do not become lawyers, and a surprising number of them never take the bar examinations. This is particularly true of the diligent young men who work their way through one of the many schools offering evening courses. The more successful and more famous law firms are looking for graduates of the major universities. They do this for two reasons: first, the graduate may be a younger man with fewer responsibilities and, hence, more willing and able to subsist on a law clerk's wages for a few years during his training; and, second, the young man is quite likely to have contacts that may be valuable to the firm at a later date.

The night school student usually cannot offer the same qualifications. His best chance for advancement can come through his employer at the time that he is going to night school. If a law degree will enable him to advance within his own company, then such effort and sacrifice can be worth while. However, the young man who fights his way through long winter evenings over a period of years with the idea of entering an established law firm may be in for a major disappointment.

However, there are many excellent opportunities for lawyers outside of the major law firms. Within the government, for example, lawyers serve not only as elected representatives in Congress but also as clerks, assistants, and aides to Congressional committees, Federal agencies, and the judicial department. And the lawyer in government has an advantage that is quite often denied his fellow civil servant. It is far easier for the lawyer to slip out of government into a well-paying business or industrial job than it is for men in most of the other civil service classifications.

As the business and the industrial world become increasingly complex and as the hand of government is felt more and more in almost every phase of American life, the role of the lawyer will increase in importance. Already, there are signs that business firms are looking more toward the legal department for top management leadership. This is a new development, and it is, perhaps, too soon to state that it is a trend. But it is only one more sign of the growing role of the lawyer on the industrial and business scene.

The Ministry

The young man who has decided upon the ministry as a career usually has made this decision on grounds that have little to do with ultimate average income figures. At the time that he decides to enter the seminary, he probably never thought about the time required to become a bishop. Usually the decision of the young ministerial student to enter the church is based on far more spiritual factors.

This does not mean that the young minister is not concerned with the practical side of life. On the contrary, the most effective minister will be a realistic man who can help the members of his congregation solve their day to day problems. Of course, he must administer to their spiritual needs, but he must, at the same time, be a practical man.

It quite often requires the same type of personality to become a successful minister that is needed to become a successful salesman or businessman. The ministry is not a place for the young man seeking a quiet shelter from the hurly-burly of life. Life has a habit of entering even the church. A minister needs drive, enthusiasm, determination, and a substantial portion of wisdom. These characteristics in any young man would be enough to insure his success in almost any field. The factor that makes a young man a minister instead of a successful insurance salesman is that intangible something that is inadequately described as the "call" to the church.

Certainly the ministry is one field where a full description of the opportunities open to the young man will have little effect on his final decision. Yet these opportunities do exist. One church group alone has announced plans to add a thousand churches to its organization within the next ten years. The shift to the suburbs has created a need for more ministers of every faith. When population increase is added to an increase in religious activity, it is little wonder that every religious group is concerned about finding enough men to staff their growing organizations. At the present time, there are 105,000,-000 Americans with some kind of church affiliation. In addition, there are millions of children who have not yet reached church membership age.

Traditionally, the minister has been poorly paid. He has been expected to take his pay in satisfaction and gratitude. This attitude is slowly changing. The salaries of ministers are being slowly raised. It should not be forgotten that a minister usually receives such "extras" as housing and an automobile allowance. The total scale of living available to the minister is not unbearable, and it shows signs of getting even better.

But ministerial work is only one of the opportunities available within the church today. Educational directors are required in the larger congregations—ministers with a background in social work are needed for work in the poorer sections of the large metropolitan areas—even men trained in psychological methods are utilized to minister to the mentally ill. The missionary is still with us. While the great area of China is closed to this activity, there is still much to be done in Africa and in South America.

Much of the above has been expressed in Protestant terms. However, both the Roman Catholic and the Jewish faiths will need well-trained, devoted men to minister to the members of their respective groups in the years ahead.

CHAPTER THIRTEEN

MAKING THE
ECONOMY TICK

"Money isn't everything" is an old adage that has little acceptance in the openly capitalistic American society in which we live. Money is the fuel that makes the economy go, and the agencies that control the flow of money are the agencies that effectively control our way of life.

The world of finance is not peopled exclusively by the tycoons and wildcat oil men. There is a place in finance for the college senior with a bent for economics and an insatiable curiosity about the complex machinery that is our free enterprise business system.

And, for the college senior with a bent for sales work, the field of finance offers some of the most lucrative jobs that a salesman could find. "Selling" money can be a very good job when it is done as a representative of an insurance company or an investment house.

Finance is big business. Not only is it big in terms of money, but it is big in terms of people. If you happen to live in a large metropolitan area with a rapidly expanding suburb, you already know that the competition among the larger banks to control the banking facilities of a new shopping center is as keen as the rivalry between oil companies for the control of the service station in that same area. Banks are expanding rapidly, both in terms of physical facilities and in terms of services offered to the customer. Paced by the more promotion-minded and aggressive banks, the banking industry has been forced to offer many new services. Many progressive banks are now in the small loan business in direct competition with the personal loan office in the same block. And this increase in service means more people in the banking business.

Although less noticeable at a casual glance, the investment houses are experiencing a similar period of growth. An investment business does not need a new building at a busy intersection in order to expand its operation. It can operate unobtrusively from any set of offices. It is the number of just such offices that are on the increase. Sparking the boom in investments has been the great surge of interest in mutual funds. Since the end of World War II, this segment of the investment scene has developed very rapidly, and some observers of the financial world are predicting that 1968 will see between 20,000 and 50,000 salesmen engaged in promoting the sale of mutual funds.

But this is not the only reason for the boom in investment houses. There has been a general increase in interest among the general public in the purchase of common stocks, bonds, and securities. Some of this activity in stocks has been brought about by a fear of inflation. Many people feel that the purchase of stocks, whose value should rise in direct proportion to the amount of inflation, is a wise form of investment. Others enter the stock market for purely speculative reasons. But, no matter what their reasons, more people are investing in stocks and bonds today than ever before in the history of the country.

The insurance field has also experienced a period of growth in the past decade. This growth has posed some rather unique problems for the industry as a whole. Insurance companies have such a tremendous supply of cash that they have considerable difficulty in finding places to invest it. This problem has already led the larger insurance companies to the point where they overshadow banks as money lenders. The search for suitable investments has led the insurance companies into the financing of housing developments, slum clearance projects, hotels, office buildings, and complete civic centers.

In some respects, the insurance companies hold forth greater promise to the college senior than do the investment houses or the banks. Insurance offers a more varied choice of activity within the business. While banks and investment houses do offer a variety of assignments, the positions offered are far from being equal in terms of potential earnings.

As the American economy grows—and all the experts predict that it will continue to grow—the role of investment houses, banks, and insurance companies in this economy will also grow. For the college senior considering a career in any one of these three fields of finance, the future could be very bright indeed.

Investment Houses

A few of the larger investment houses recruit college seniors on the campus. These are the organizations with branch offices in cities across the country. Those that do recruit seniors move the new employee directly into a training program lasting from eight to twelve months. The concentration in these training courses is mainly in sales techniques, and the student entering one of them may become quite bored with his studies before the end of the indoctrination period.

He will find that sales techniques are rather elementary stuff after his college courses in market analysis, economic theory, and corporate structure.

A different type of training program is offered by a few investment houses. This one consists of a few months in each of the four main sections of the organization. A college graduate may be first assigned to the buying department where he will analyze the financial condition of a given company, study its management, and make a full report to his supervisor. From there he will move successively through the underwriting and syndication sections, observing the functioning of each before finally being shifted into the sales section.

However, the large investment houses are only a part of the total investment picture. Every city of any size has one or more investment houses where a young man can get a start. In applying for such a local position it is only realistic to point out that personal connections will count far more than a "B" average in economic theory. This does not mean that local investment houses are looking for sub-par students. It does mean that this type of work is generally considered to be long on prestige value, and the young man with good connections in the community has a running start on a successful career in this field. Prestige and salary—at least for beginners—are usually in inverse proportion and this rule holds at investment houses. The pay for a young man beginning in this field is going to be much less than other positions in either business or industry, and, when compared with the starting salary for a young engineer, the pay for a new employee in the investment business appears almost ludicrous.

However, there is another semi-mathematical rule involving prestige. Where there is high prestige, there is also high potential. A salesman in an investment house can, through commissions, earn a thoroughly respectable living. And his contacts, usually with the business and financial leaders of the community, can be of even greater value to him.

But this potential exists only in the customer-contact or sales end of the investment business. The salaries paid for highly trained men in the statistical or analytical phases of the business are likely to be slightly less than those paid for similar work in industry. The great opportunities are in sales.

Sales work within an investment house utilizes a decidedly "soft" sell technique. The concept of the fast talker peddling bogus or risky stocks over the telephone went out with the '29 crash, and, while some "boiler shops" still operate, they are far from the rule. A customer-contact man in the conservative investment house—and most investment houses are very conservative—must build customer confidence by supplying his buyers with sound advice about the stock market. The ability to give sound advice can come only from a thorough knowledge of the market and its day-to-day activity.

In this customer-contact work, personality must be mixed with ability. The combination in a young man can spell success in the investment business.

At the present time, many of the local investment houses are family operations that are carryovers from the more wide-open financial climate of the end of the nineteenth century. The success of some of the national investment houses has lent some credence to the prediction that some of these traditionally family operations will be forced to merge. Should this occur within the next ten years, it will mean greater opportunity for the college graduate without an inside connection to move into the field. A large investment house is less personal and more apt to hire solely on the applicant's record.

All of this indicates that there is definite room for advancement within the banking business. It does not mean that the advancement in terms of salary will be equivalent to advancement in terms of job title. The variation in salary structure between one bank and another can be very great, and it is very difficult for a young man, on the outside, to gain any clear picture of this structure at the time he is considering a position with any given bank. The banking business is also a relatively stable one, and it is seldom possible for a young man to improve himself by moving from one job to another— a practice that works very well in the case of the young engineer.

As in the investment business, the ancillary functions of the banking business offer low salaries, and clerking and accounting jobs are poorly rewarded.

However, even the small local banks are beginning to realize that they must train top-caliber people to take over administrative posts. At the present time, there are training programs in the form of correspondence courses sponsored by the state banking association in all of the states. These courses are offered at both the clerical and the supervisory level. In several large cities, more formalized programs are offered by the American Institute of Banking. It is only a matter of time before full-scale training programs and a concentrated search for alert young college graduates to enter these programs will be initiated by local banks.

Banking opportunities also include trust administration, both for individuals and for institutions. This is a growing field of interest for many banks, and the men chosen for such posts are properly compensated. Moreover, large banking operations, involved in a measure of foreign commerce, require top caliber young men to fill positions both in this country and overseas. As American trade expands, this is certain to become a major factor in the total business picture of many banks.

Insurance

There is no other way to describe the insurance business except to say that it is big. It is big in the types of insurance companies in the field, big in the number of insurance companies of each type, big in the amount of money involved, big in the number of people involved, and big in opportunity for young men just leaving college.

MAKING THE ECONOMY TICK

Banking

Recruiting on the college campus is done by only twelve o[r]
teen of the largest commercial banks. Young men entering
organizations can count on good starting salaries and a tr[aining]
program lasting from a year to twenty-six months. This rec[ruiting]
on the campus is likely to be confined to the geographic area[s]
by their centers of operation. For example, a New York ban[k]
go to schools in New England, New Jersey, and New York
but it is not likely to carry its recruiting into Ohio or Ma[ine]

A young man entering one of these larger banks will h[ave an]
A.B. degree and will receive a starting salary in the neighborh[ood of]
$4,500 a year. A few students with M.A. degrees are also rec[ruited]
and the starting salary for these young men may go as h[igh as]
$6,000. The training program will consist of both formal cla[ss]
instruction and a tour of duty in each of the major sections
bank.

These salaries appear quite attractive, and they do, in fac[t, com]
pare favorably with those paid in industry and other section[s of the]
business world. However, the young man cannot expect th[at this]
salary pattern will be repeated at every bank in the country.
of the positions in the banking business—and there are 650,0[00]
positions—are at the community level where the pay scale
comparable with that of the larger banks mentioned above.
local banks do not recruit on the campus, and training progr[am are]
almost unheard of in the great majority of these organizati[ons. In]
fact, some banks are not even interested in hiring college gra[duates]
and, when they do, the pay is extremely poor. For example, [in]
metropolitan areas, the young man with five to eight years o[f bank]
ing experience, who is assigned to the manager's post of a su[burban]
branch office, will be paid a salary comparable to that of [an]
engineer in his first year with an airframe company.

Local banks have been able to maintain this salary patt[ern be]
cause they have offered security and some measure of p[restige.]
There are a great number of officer posts within any given [bank]
operation. In a small bank, there may be one officer to ev[ery]
workers. In a larger bank, the ratio may be one officer to e[very]
workers. And because there are so many supervisory pos[ts,]
openings for officers arise at the rate of one thousand a yea[r.]

Most of the large insurance companies do recruit on the campus, and their needs are not limited to business administration majors and potential salesmen. The New York Life Insurance Company even recruits electrical engineers and provides a training program for the college graduates to teach them programming and operation of large scale data processing equipment. Insurance companies are large enough to require fully staffed personnel departments and are actively seeking recruits for this type of work. Mathematicians are needed in the actuarial sections, and the training period for college graduates in this activity can last as long as nine years.

The big central offices of the major insurance companies are tremendous papermills, daily producing thousands of printed records that must be processed and filed. This work requires men with business administration background and men with training in systems and procedures. And, of course, accountants are needed in large numbers.

But the greatest need in every insurance operation is for good, hard-working salesmen. Insurance is a highly competitive field, and the insurance plans offered for sale by one company are likely to differ only in detail from those offered by their competitors. For this reason, every major insurance company conducts extensive training programs for young men about to enter its sales department, and this training continues throughout the man's working career with the company.

Insurance sales work covers a multitude of activities from collecting a 25-cent a week debit in a poor neighborhood to the sale of multi-million dollar plans covering the employees of a large corporation. The insurance field is represented by both the fast talking, slick huckster and the calm, analytical, thoughtful man who bases his sales talk on closely reasoned arguments. For this reason, it is impossible to generalize about insurance sales work. It is literally a field that offers an opportunity for a great variety of young men of different personality and background.

The return for insurance sales work is surprisingly good. Young men who have known friends and acquaintances who have taken up insurance sales as a part-time job may have obtained the mistaken impression that such work does not pay well enough to warrant a man's working full-time at it. Such is far from the case. The man who puts an honest effort into full time insurance selling can do extremely well.

The young man who enters the field of insurance selling is not likely to earn big money during his first few years on the job, and, for some time, his wages may compare unfavorably with some other activity, such as engineering. Insurance sales is work that is some time in developing. It requires a long period of customer cultivation and of building confidence in the customer for the advice and counsel of the salesman. The peak of insurance salesmanship is achieved when a salesman has brought a customer along to the point where he simply calls the salesman, states his need for a given type of coverage, and waits for the salesman to deliver the policy. At this point, the salesman functions in a manner similar to the family doctor or lawyer.

Insurance sales is often a way for a young man to go into business for himself at a relatively early period in his life. While many men earn fine incomes by representing a single insurance company, others find it profitable to branch out and handle the insurance sales of a number of companies in a given area. For example, a man may contract to sell the automobile insurance of one company, the life insurance of another, and the casualty insurance of a third. In this manner, he may become an independent businessman in his own city or town.

Insurance sales to individuals is far from the only type of work available to a salesman in this field. One of the choice assignments is that of selling group health insurance, group life insurance, and pension plans to large corporations. This type of sales work can literally involve millions of dollars, and the "sell" is conducted in a serious, businesslike atmosphere. Needless to say, the men assigned to such work are considered by their employers to be the best insurance men in the business, and the compensation granted them fully reflects this high opinion of their ability.

A man concerned with the sale of group insurance plans to corporations will probably hold a high position within the insurance company and could, quite conceivably, be an officer. As a rule, he will operate from the company's main office and will do considerable traveling to contact potential customers in other parts of the country. In most cases, he will not be concerned with the sale of other insurance, even though his company may offer a full range of insurance services.

But sales work is not the only attractive position in the insurance field for the college graduate. A math major with an interest in business will find real opportunity in the actuarial departments of the major insurance firms. These departments are charged with the responsibility of setting up the table of rates for the insurance policies offered for sale by the company. This is demanding work, requiring a long period of training and considerable experience. The young man who succeeds in completing the arduous training program set up for men in this field will find himself in an excellent position within the company. These are well paying positions that compare very favorably with similar posts in industry.

As a general rule, the insurance companies tend to pay somewhat better salaries all the way down the line for office administration positions than does industry. In a manufacturing plant, the office force is an ancillary function of the assembly line, but, in the insurance company, the office force is the important unit. The only "product" produced by an insurance firm is "paperwork," and the administrators of the big companies have learned the value of having top caliber people on their staffs to insure efficient handling of that "paperwork." For this reason, some of the better positions open to business administration graduates are with the major insurance companies. In addition to offering security and pleasant working conditions, the central offices of the larger insurance firms are likely to be located in major metropolitan areas, making it possible for a college graduate to continue his education through additional study at night.

Because of their pressing problem to find new areas in which to invest the large sums of money in their control, the insurance companies have invaded many of the fields formerly the sole province of the banking business. Many companies are now active in the home mortgage field and, of course, their investment portfolios have grown to very sizable proportions. In this latter activity, the insurance companies require personnel similar to that required by the investment business. The economics major with an interest in the stock market but with no desire to become a salesman of stocks and bonds may find a real opportunity in this phase of the insurance business.

The growing scope of the insurance operation has created the need for a great number of specialists whose job titles are far removed from the traditional concept of the insurance business. The tremendous investment of the larger companies in slum clearance projects, city center construction, and housing developments has involved them in city planning, social welfare, and population studies. However, these specialists, when utilized by the insurance companies, usually come from outside of the insurance field.

It is difficult to say exactly what makes a good salesman. Certainly there is no one college course that a young man should take to make certain that he will be a success in the field. While it is hardly definitive to say that a good salesman should have "personality" and that he should "like people," there seems to be no other way in which to phrase it. There is no reason why an English or a history major could not be a good insurance salesman, and there is no reason to assume that because a young man has majored in business he will be good at the job. Courses in psychology might be of some help, but they are not mandatory. There is no set pattern of training.

Insurance sales work should be investigated by a liberal arts major who is undecided about his future. This is not to say that he should look upon insurance sales work as a last resort. On the contrary, no man should enter any field unless he is reasonably sure that he will enjoy his work. However, a thorough study of the opportunities available in insurance may uncover a number of pleasant surprises for the young man who has not heretofore given much thought to the subject.

There is yet another phase of work in the insurance field that remains to be discussed. Large corporations have extensive insurance requirements, both for their personnel and for their plant facilities. In a corporation with plants scattered all across the country, the varieties of fire insurance, accident insurance, workman's compensation insurance, weather damage insurance and what-have-you that may be required by the laws of a dozen states can be very great. In addition, a corporation may be involved in group life and group health insurance plans for its employees. In some cases a corporate pension plan may also be carried by an insurance company.

The magnitude of this operation may require that a corporation maintain an insurance officer to oversee the administration of this vast insurance program. This is a responsible position that carries with it an excellent salary. And, while it is hardly a post to which a college senior can aspire in his few years out of school, it is worth noting as another excellent possibility in the insurance field.

A "yes" answer to the first question is necessary for every student going into graduate school. A "yes" answer to the second question will help the senior decide whether the sacrifice in time and money is warranted.

For most graduate students, the period of time required to get an advanced degree is one of the most financially trying periods of their lives. It is the time when they are likely to meet the girl whom they want to marry—and they do marry. It is the time of living in small apartments, of eating out of cans, of feeling guilty about spending the price of a movie. It is a time of trying to study or write with a newborn baby crying in the same room. It means part-time jobs, working all summer, and baby sitting while the wife holds down yet another part-time job. For the great majority of students, graduate school calls for real sacrifice.

Why do they do it?

It is true that the Ph.D. in physics, for example, will be able to command $8,500 or more upon graduation instead of the $6,000 that he would have gotten with his A.B. five years earlier. But it is fair to state that his Ph.D. has cost him between thirty and forty thousand dollars.

Why do they make the sacrifice?

The young man who has a real thirst for knowledge—who wants to find out for himself how and why the world is as it is—can be satisfied with nothing less than full understanding.

From a financial standpoint, graduate school must be appraised as a long-term investment. While the starting salary for a man with an advanced degree is quite likely to be greater than that of a man with an A.B., it must be remembered that it takes several years to obtain the advanced degree—years in which the graduate student is earning little or nothing.

When all the arithmetic is done, the Ph.D. candidate in physics realizes that he will be in his forties before he fully catches up with the monetary loss that he suffered while going through graduate school. At graduation, even with his Ph.D., his salary is approximately that of the A.B. who has been working in industry. It is true that he can look forward to a better salary in later years, but this is hard to reconcile when he has been working for almost nothing and living in one room for years. And, with a little luck, the

A.B. will always stay ahead of the Ph.D.'s salary. After all, he has had five years to learn the politics of his company. He may have had the opportunity to switch to administration, and he could, quite conceivably, become the boss of the Ph.D.

In the sciences, engineering, teaching, and the more specialized areas, such as industrial relations, business administration, or business management, the graduate student can clearly foresee how he will use the training that he is obtaining through advanced study. But for the humanities student who does not expect to teach, the advantages are not so apparent.

For the student who has decided to become a doctor, a lawyer, or a minister, the decision on graduate school has already been made. These professions require advanced education, and the student is well aware of this fact when he makes one of them his choice for a lifetime career.

There are other occupations that make equally strong, though less formal, demands for graduate study. The future college professor knows that he must obtain at least an M.A. degree, and preferably a Ph.D., if he is to advance in his calling. Fortunately for the student, the colleges and the universities make it possible to teach on a part-time basis while graduate study is in progress.

Teaching

In recent years it has become almost mandatory that the public school teacher obtain graduate education if he expects to obtain increased income and increased responsibilities within the school system. In fact, the student who wishes to go right from college to teaching in a high school classroom will find that the M.A. is the minimum requirement for such an assignment in a number of communities. A year of graduate study is absolutely essential for this student.

The public school teacher in a metropolitan area may find that it is more practical to leave college with his A.B. and to depend upon the afternoon and evening courses of the local university for his advanced work. For the student from a less urban area, when such graduate education is not readily available, an extra full year of graduate study may prove to pay real dividends in terms of salary and assignments. The education student should carefully check the graduate course requirements of his school system and evaluate his future course of action on the basis of the availability of graduate education resources in his area.

Of one thing, however, the education student may be certain. At some time in his teaching career, he must be prepared to do graduate work.

Science

The science student with a desire to do basic research work must also be prepared to spend two or more years in graduate school. The very bulk of the material that must be mastered by the research-scientist makes it impossible for a man to be trained in the four years of undergraduate school. In research laboratories within industry, an M.A. is generally considered to be minimal, while the Ph.D. is the more common requirement.

Since a great deal of the pure research being carried on in the United States is being done at universities, the graduate student benefits greatly. This means that the Ph.D. candidate in physics or chemistry or biology can obtain part-time employment at the university at the time he is completing his degree requirements. Often it is possible for the thesis work to be a part of one of the university's research projects. The student may find himself in a position where he is actually paid for his study. Unfortunately, this situation is common only in the sciences. The history, geography, or sociology student can seldom count upon an income from any source while completing his graduate work.

Engineering

In engineering, the advanced degree can be turned directly into monetary advantage. Higher wages are paid to men with an M.A. or a Ph.D. Many companies make it a specific policy to encourage their men to attend evening classes in graduate work, and many actually pay all or part of the expenses of such training. No engineer should consider his college work complete with the B.S. degree. And in selecting a company to work for, the student will be very wise to find one that has a working graduate training program with a local university.

The demand for advanced degrees in engineering is of post-war origin, and it is a constantly accelerating demand. The student who finds that it is financially feasible to take an M.A. before going in search of an engineering job will find that the monetary rewards are worthwhile. Perhaps in no other field can the rewards of graduate training be realized as quickly as they can be in engineering.

In the manufacturing end of industry, including the areas of industrial engineering and production engineering, the graduate degree is the exception and not the rule. These occupations have not yet reached the point where they can absorb graduate level courses in these areas, and the companies actively seeking such graduates are the exception and not the rule. It will take another five or ten years and the introduction of much more automation equipment into all phases of industry before graduate education becomes the accepted standard in these phases of production.

Government

The nation as a whole is becoming more and more education conscious. At the present time, the A.B. degree is required for many positions which only a few decades ago were filled with high-school graduates. The pattern set by the public education field is rapidly being adapted for use by other professions. For example, it is not at all unusual for a state or a municipality to require an M.A. for its better assignments in social work.

Within the Federal government, a salary schedule has been developed that is based, in part, upon graduate education. In Washington no less than four universities run extensive graduate evening schools in order to meet the demand of government workers for courses which will enable them to increase their earning power through the acquisition of graduate degrees. Even within the armed services, an officer with an administrator's assignment will find that his chances of advancing from captain to major can be improved if he obtains an M.A. in business management or in personnel administration.

Undoubtedly, some of this enthusiasm for advanced work is misplaced. But the graduate degree has become a yardstick, however inadequate, that large industries and big government agencies can use to measure the worth of their employees. Present indications are that neither industry nor government have any plans to develop substitute yardsticks, and the demand for graduate education can only increase.

Sales

However, in many occupations experience is still the best teacher. Within the large sales organizations, the A.B. may be required for the initial position, but after that the sales chart becomes a more efficient yardstick than the graduate degree. Here business does have a measuring device that admirably suits its purposes. The student with the M.A. who elects to go into sales work will soon find that his additional study will be of little use to him if his sales-book is not regularly filled with orders.

Within the research departments of the bigger sales organizations, statisticians, sociologists, and psychologists may find the advanced degree does help to qualify for a good position. But these jobs are few when compared to the great number of sales assignments within the same company.

Advertising

In the advertising business the story is the same. The graduate student will find that he is judged solely on his work, and the additional intellectual background that he obtained in graduate school is of little use. In fact, the advertising business is still one of the few businesses where the advanced degree is looked upon with a jaundiced eye. Advertising people lay great stress on experience, and they have a fear that the more highly trained graduate student will have lost some of his creative flare and his ability to attack problems from new and unorthodox directions. In terms of salary, a graduate degree is unlikely to pay real dividends in the advertising business except in specialized positions. For example, in the growing research side of advertising, the advanced degree is encouraged. This is true in part because the advertising agencies want the prestige of a battery of graduate degree holders in order to impress clients with the worth of their research sections.

Business Administration

With the possible exception of education, no phase of undergraduate education has grown faster than the schools of business. The increasing demand for graduate education in business administration would seem to indicate that industry was bestowing vast rewards upon young men with graduate training in this subject.

However, a 1955 survey by Business Week magazine indicated that very few top executives had any graduate education at all, although a large majority of them had gone to college.

Perhaps it is too soon to measure the effect of graduate training in business administration on business itself. One thing appears obvious, however. The demand for graduate business training is generated as much by the students as it is by industry.

With the growth of large and, in some cases, excellent graduate schools of business, industry has resorted to sending some of its top management and middle management people back to school for short courses. However, only in rare cases does industry grant a man time to get a full degree. And the practice is far from universal. Many small companies and a good many large ones still feel that experience is the best teacher.

The support of graduate education that is thrust upon engineers is only grudgingly handed out to members of the accounting department or to members of the general administrative staff. There are, of course, exceptions, such as General Electric which makes it possible for its administrative people to have the same graduate education opportunities as engineers, but this practice is not widespread.

All of this leads to the belief that industry has simply not had time to appreciate all of the implications of a fully developed system of graduate education for aspiring young executives. It is probably only a matter of time before these schools become integrated into the business world in the same manner that the graduate education schools have become a fixture in education.

At the present time, however, the worth of graduate training in business administration to an individual student will depend largely upon the company for which he chooses to go to work. Some large businesses already lay great store in the graduate degree. To others the advanced degree means little or nothing.

The student interested in graduate business education will likely gravitate toward those companies seeking graduate students, while the A.B. in business administration will naturally seek out the concerns that lay stress on graduate work. To the individual, the geographic considerations of his employment are likely to be the deciding factor. If the companies in his area demand extra schooling, then he would be wise to attend graduate school. If his area is not interested in graduates from schools of business, then two more years in college could well be a waste of time—at least from a monetary standpoint.

The Humanities

The history major, who as a senior becomes wrapped up in the fine points of English history and goes on to graduate school to major in that subject, is literally throwing away thousands of dollars. He may have a good job awaiting him in his uncle's office or his father's business, but, first, he must pursue his thirst for knowledge. This attitude is the despair of his parents and the joy of his instructors. At the end of his graduate study, the young man may well accept the job in the family firm—to the relief of his parents and the sorrow of his professors.

Such devotion to his studies may seem foolish to everyone but the student. Actually, such an attitude is no different than that of the physics Ph.D. who does see some form of monetary gain on the horizon, no matter how distant. Both study because they must.

The student of English history has not wasted his time in graduate school. It is true that the year 1066 and the accurate tabulation of the monarchs of England and Scotland will be of little use in his family's plastic manufacturing company. But the young man will have learned how to research a problem, evaluate facts, and reach a conclusion. Such abilities are not wasted in any profession. He will also, through the medium of innumerable term papers and his thesis, learn how to express himself in writing—an essential for any executive. The discipline of graduate school is good for any man.

But what of the young man who does not have the family business to fall back upon? Can the monetary loss incurred by attending graduate school ever be made up?

In this case, graduate school becomes a real gamble. Certainly the young man will benefit intellectually. He will gain a cultural background that will enable him to get more out of art, music, literature, and life. But, in terms of salary, it is doubtful that graduate school can be justified. It is true that the Ph.D. is far better equipped to compete in the business world than is the A.B., but he comes to the scene five years later. He must pit his advanced training against men with five years of practical experience in the same job. This is a difficult handicap to overcome.

The evaluation of the Ph.D. must be made in personal terms, and this is something that must be done by the individual.

The Ph.D. also has some social value, even in industrial circles. This is not to suggest that the student obtain a Ph.D. in order to obtain social status. It does suggest, however, that the Ph.D. training makes a man stand out from the normal patterns of industry—and from the normal patterns of society.

The graduate student is, in many ways, like the man who decides to become a teacher. He knows that his course of action involves sacrifice and that he, very likely, will never make a great deal of money, but it is something that he must do because he would not be happy doing anything else.

Even within the occupations that lay great stress on graduate training, such as education, government, and social work, the graduate degree is no automatic ticket to economic paradise. In every case the man will have to produce within the framework of his assignment. In these fields the degree helps, but it does not solve all problems.

If the decision on whether or not a student should go to graduate school must be boiled down to a single question, the decision should be made on whether or not the student really and truly wants to learn more about a particular area of knowledge.

CHAPTER FIFTEEN

MORE THAN A SHOE SHINE

THE TWENTY-MINUTE interview warrants a great deal of preparation on the part of the college senior. And this preparation should go far beyond a clean shirt, polished shoes, and combed hair. It goes without saying that the student should appear for an interview neatly dressed, but it is unnecessary for him to appear looking as if he had just stepped out of an *Esquire* fashion layout. The college recruiter is interested in more important things than the depth of an applicant's wardrobe.

And, just as the recruiter is interested in more than the Ivy cut of the applicant's clothes, the senior should be in a position to judge the recruiter's company by more than the personality of the man sent to the campus to conduct the fateful twenty-minute interviews.

Preparing for the Interview

By the time the student reaches his senior year and begins to look forward to the years ahead in business or in industry, he should have a pretty good idea of what he wants to do. Unfortunately, this is not always the case. Many young men reach this stage in their lives without any clean-cut concept of what they intend to do with their lives.

It is time that they found out.

A good place to start to find the answer to this problem is with the senior's counselor or with a favorite professor. These men have had an opportunity to observe the student throughout his college career and are in a position to evaluate objectively the strengths and weaknesses of an individual college senior. A frank discussion with these men can be of great assistance.

For example, assume that a senior is in his last year of an electrical engineering course. This man could go to work for a company that places heavy emphasis on product research and development, for one that stresses straight product engineering, or for one that requires engineering personnel for the operation and maintenance of its facilities. A professor who has seen literally hundreds of students and who knows how past graduates have fared in industry can tell a senior if he is strong enough in the theoretical side of his studies to attempt a research assignment or if his talents are more in the line of product engineering. It is almost impossible for the student himself to answer these questions with objectivity.

An English professor can tell one of his seniors if he has enough writing ability to tackle newspaper work, to write advertising copy, or to write novels. A history professor knows his students well enough to be able to advise them whether or not to seek work in the business world or to go on to graduate school.

A request for this kind of help will not be considered an imposition by the professor. The teacher who coldly grades papers and sends these grades to the registrar's office is far from cold when it comes to the real interests of his students. In almost every case, a senior will find his professors not only able but willing to counsel him in the choice of a career in which he will be able to use his talents to best advantage.

A second source of information for the college senior is the group of alumni who graduated into business and industry the previous June. By recalling the personalities and the abilities of the students who went into different fields, the senior may be able to draw some close parallels with his own case. If the senior has the opportunity to talk to alumni who have spent several years in the working world, he will gain additional data about specific careers in specific companies.

A third source of information—and a most important one—is the college placement officer. This man has daily contact, year in and year out, with both college seniors seeking careers in industry and business and with representatives of industry and business seeking college graduates to man their expanding operations.

The Interview Itself

The twenty-minute interview is of great importance to the college senior, and it is just as important to the college recruiter. The student is bargaining for a career while the recruiter is forced to decide whether or not to invest his company's time and money in an unknown young man.

Three things happen in an interview:

1. The recruiter attempts to convince the student that his company offers great opportunities and is an ideal place to work.
2. The student attempts to convince the recruiter that he is an alert, able, willing young man with great drive and initiative. In short, he is exactly the type of college graduate that this particular company needs.
3. The recruiter makes up his mind whether or not to hire this particular student. (Fortunately, for the student, he is not faced with an immediate choice. Should an offer be made, he may reserve his final decision until after he has compared all other offers.)

There is no set pattern to the interview, but because twenty minutes is not a long period of time, the recruiter must begin to make up his mind about a college senior almost from the minute that he walks into the room.

But how does the student sell himself to a recruiter?

It can be assumed that the student's grades are a matter of record. His transcript is normally available to the interviewer or at least the interviewer is able to obtain an idea of the student's general academic standing from the placement officer. There is little that a senior can do at this point to change the record of the past four years.

The student's efforts must be directed toward proving to the recruiter that he is an alert, intelligent young man. This does not mean that he should be over-aggressive, nor does it mean that he should appear to be a super-sophisticate with a diffident manner. There is no trick to appearing alert. All the student need do is look interested in what the recruiter is telling him, give good concise answers to any questions, and be prepared to ask some sensible questions himself.

One thing is most important. He must pay close attention to everything that the recruiter tells him. Nothing creates a worse impression than for the recruiter to have to repeat something that he has already explained.

What kind of questions should the senior ask?

Since all interviews are certain to differ, it is impossible to provide the student with a fixed "pony" for the twenty-minute interview. The questions asked by the student will depend upon how well the recruiter has explained his company's policies and how comprehensive was the literature supplied in advance of the interview.

Below are some of the things that the college senior will need to know in order to intelligently evaluate any offer that he might receive:

1. Is there a training program for college graduates? If so, how long does it last?
2. What will be my first assignment within the company, and what can I expect my next assignment to be?
3. Assuming that I prove to be good on the job, what can I expect my progress to be in the next five years with your company?
4. What are the advantages of working for your company rather than for your chief competitor?
5. Do you make it possible for college graduates to work toward an advanced academic degree? If so, does the company pay any part of the cost of graduate study?
6. Will I have to move at any time after joining the company? Will I be expected to do much traveling?
7. Does your company have an automatic salary increase program, a merit increase program, or both?
8. Is it possible for me to change my speciality once I am working for the company?
9. What is your (the recruiter's) own history with the company?
10. What are the opportunities within your company for the humanities student?

Of course, it will not be necessary for every college senior to ask every one of these questions. Some of them may not even apply. They are listed here simply as a guide.

There are two other factors that the college senior must learn about any company. Both concern the somewhat delicate subject of money. Of course, the starting salary on any job is going to be of great importance to a graduating student. Yet the student must not overlook the fact that he should also search the interviewer's sales talk for data about the total opportunity picture within the company. And, above all, he must not give the impression that his only concern is with the immediate dollar return of a particular job. It is perfectly all right to ask the direct question, "What do you pay a starting college graduate for this type of work?" But the question should be followed up immediately with questions about how much the student will be able to earn after five years on the job and what job title he can expect to have at the end of the same period. This line of questioning will not only elicit information that the student needs in order to make a fully reasoned choice of a position, but it is also good "politics" for the sake of the interview.

Of equal importance is the student's attitude toward the fringe benefits. For a senior of twenty-one or twenty-two years of age to show an inordinate interest in pension plans, indicates to the recruiter that this man is more concerned with job security than with opportunity. Again it is permissible to ask about life insurance or pension plans, but the point should not be labored.

Often, a recruiter will request that the student submit a résumé of his past work history (if any), his scholastic activities, his extracurricular activities, and his personal interests. This is something that the student should do as a matter of course. Even if his campus interviews do not demand a résumé, he will need one for the mail inquiries to firms that do not send a recruiter to the campus.

The preparation of a résumé requires considerable thought. It is not something to be dashed off between classes. Even experienced executives with many years in business and industry behind them sometimes turn the job of preparing a résumé over to a professional firm of résumé writers. However, for the college senior, such drastic measures are not necessary. But a little work is in order.

The résumé should contain pertinent information such as age, height, weight, space for a snapshot portrait, address, telephone number (both at college and at home), and marital and draft board status.

The student's major at college should be listed along with any minor or specialized courses. If the student finished in the upper 10 per cent or 25 per cent of his class, he should say so.

This should be followed by a statement of the student's immediate and long-term employment aims.

His previous work history should be listed. This list should include summer jobs or part-time work performed during the school year to help defray college expenses. Even if the student is looking for a post as an engineer, it is not amiss to list waiting on tables or life-guarding at a resort as work experience. Of course, a summer in a drafting room of an engineering office is more impressive than a summer as a counselor at a boy's camp. But the counseling job is better than no job at all. Personnel departments realize that the opportunities for summer work are often limited. And, quite often, a routine job can have real value. For example, a summer in a supermarket would not be wasted for a young man going into the advertising business.

Next in line for the résumé should come a list of college activities. Social fraternities, honorary fraternities, athletics, dramatics, student newspaper, ROTC, or what have you. If the student held office in any of these activities, this should be mentioned along with any real responsibilities carried during the term of office. For example, if the student were in charge of the Junior Prom, this indicates that he has displayed an ability to organize and carry out a sizable project.

Even if extracurricular activities in college had no other value (and, of course, they do have other values), they would be important solely for their use in building an impressive résumé. This should be followed by a perfunctory list of hobbies and outside interests.

This chapter contains a sample résumé for a hypothetical liberal arts student interested in obtaining a position in the personnel department of a large corporation.

At the end of the twenty-minute interview, the recruiter will probably have reached a decision about the college senior. He may extend an offer immediately, or, more likely, he will tell the young man that the home office will write to him within a few days.

Once the college senior has finished his schedule of interviews, he reaches a point when it is his turn to make a decision. Let us assume that a senior is fortunate enough to have five or six offers made to him by recruiters on the campus. In addition, he may have an offer or two as a result of the contacts he has made on his own off the campus. This may sound overly optimistic, but in the boom years of 1955, 1956, and 1957 many young engineers were in this enviable position.

The senior should notify the company of his choice as soon as possible. This should be done for two reasons: first, it is the right and polite thing to do; and, second, the student who stalls several months on his decision may find that the company of his choice has filled its quota of college seniors for the year. It also creates a poor impression for the student to procrastinate for months, and no personnel department is going to think well of a young man who puts off making a final decision or who evades their queries for a final answer.

While a decision should be made as soon as possible and the company notified just as promptly, the student should remember that his decision is not irrevocable. In extenuating circumstances, he may withdraw his commitment to report to a given company. This last statement should not be taken as advice to string along two or more companies. Recruiting agents and personnel people have professional societies and meetings where this sort of tactic soon becomes a topic of conversation. A mark of this kind on a man's record can do his career little good within the company for which he finally goes to work.

It is quite possible that a student can become confused by a multiplicity of offers. If he is genuinely undecided about a specific company, he may legitimately request a trip to visit the firm's office or plant. Many organizations will pay a prospective employee's expenses on a trip of this type.

It is also inevitable that the subject of careers and interviews will become a part of Student Union bull sessions. Up to a point, the comments of fellow students will be helpful to the senior. But, in the final analysis, he will have to make his own decision.

The interview Comparison Check-List, included in this chapter, may be of some help in arriving at a decision. The chart contains a listing of the major factors affecting a student's final choice. It does not list them all because every case is different and a point of vital interest to one student may be of no importance to another.

For the same reason, the chart can give no relative "weight" or point value to any given factor. For example, the availability of graduate study may be of great importance to an engineer and of almost no value to a young man entering sales work.

To use this chart, the student simply fills in the name of each company making him an offer in the spaces across the top of the chart. He then fills in, as fully as possible, the answers to the questions in the left-hand column.

But, even when all the spaces are filled in, the student must make his own decision.

And it is an important one.

Good luck!

INTERVIEW COMPARISON CHECK-LIST

	Company X Detroit Michigan	Company Y	Company Z
Training program available	Yes		
How long is training program?	One year		
Graduate study possible	Yes		
Will company assist?	No		
Starting salary	$4,500		
Possible Salary in five years	$7,500		
Possible position in five years	No commitment		
Merit increases for salary	Yes		
Benefits — Life insurance	Yes		
Benefits — Pension plan	Eligible after one year with company		
Benefits — Hospitalization and Major Medical	Fully paid by company		
Will I have to travel?	No		
Will I have to move?	Yes		

SAMPLE RÉSUMÉ

HOWARD W. JONES

Present Address:	Room 1215 Alumni Memorial Hall Johns Hopkins University Baltimore 18, Maryland HOpkins 7-3300, Ext 712
Home Address:	1836 Chestnut Street Willowdale, North Carolina PErkins 5-2030
Personal Data:	Height: 5'10" Weight: 165 pounds Age: 22 Marital Status: Single Draft: ROTC Reserve Officer
Professional Data:	Position in personnel section of middle- to large-sized corporation. Position should lead to work at a later date in the field of labor relations.
Educational Background:	High School: Willowdale High School, Willowdale, North Carolina. General Academic Course, graduated 1955. College: A.B. Johns Hopkins University 1959. Major in psychology. Additional courses in history, economics and labor relations.
Work History:	Summer 1955: Clerk in supermarket, Willowdale, North Carolina. Summer 1956: Counselor, Beaver Day Camp, Rocky Mount, North Carolina. 1956-57 (part time) clerk, Alumni Records Office, Johns Hopkins University. Maintaining personnel history file of University graduate student alumni. Summer 1957: Counselor, Beaver Day Camp, Rocky Mount, North Carolina. 1957-58 (part time) clerk, Alumni Records Office, Johns Hopkins University. Summer 1958: Guide, Smoky Mountain National Park. Employed in central office, planning tours for parties of tourists.

College Activities:

Social Fraternity: Delta Upsilon
Treasurer in junior and senior years.
Honorary Fraternity: O.D.K.
Awarded membership for participation in student activities.
Student Newspaper: Feature writer in junior and senior years.
Athletics: J.V. basketball as freshman and sophomore. Varsity track as junior and senior.
Glee Club: Member for four years.
Vice-president as junior, president as senior. Responsible as president for planning and execution of eighteen concert-schedule covering three states. Glee Club had 55 members.
Inter-Fraternity Board: Member for two years.
Honor Commission: Member for one year.

Hobbies and Interests:

Music and collecting high-fidelity recordings. Hunting and camping.

C